GW00982993

7

Primary School
Management

Primary School Management

ROY JONES

David & Charles
Newton Abbot   London   North Pomfret (Vt)

British Library Cataloguing in Publication Data
Jones, Roy
  Primary school management.
  1. Elementary school principals – Great
  Britain
  I. Title
  372.1'2'0120941   LB2822.5

        ISBN 0-7153-7843-0

          © Roy Jones 1980

Set by Northern Phototypesetting Co, Bolton, Lancashire
and printed in Great Britain
by Redwood Burn Ltd., Trowbridge, Wiltshire
for David & Charles (Publishers) Limited
Brunel House, Newton Abbot, Devon

Published in the United States of America
by David & Charles Inc
North Pomfret, Vermont 05053, USA

Contents

To Christopher and Catherine

Introduction

This book is intended for headteachers and aspiring headteachers of primary schools who take their management role and its application to planning seriously. No one would doubt that the education service will continue to be in the forefront of public activity and scrutiny during the eighties. For the past fifteen years the centre of the education stage has been taken by the debate on reorganisation of secondary education on comprehensive lines. A time of consolidation is now needed in those schools and it is probable that other parts of the service will come in to the limelight. There is a growing debate about the needs of the sixteen-to-nineteen age-group while the Warnock Report has encouraged a rethinking about the education of children with special needs. The primary school is unlikely to be forgotten and headteachers will be in the frontline of discussion and debate.

There have always been, and no doubt always will be, critics of primary schools. Too often they are people with little direct knowledge of infant and junior education. Even if they have some knowledge there is frequently less understanding of the reasoning, methods and results achieved by the schools. Accountability is now the fashionable word, increasingly used without meaning, and the primary head in the eighties can expect the community at large to be more interested and more questioning than in the past. The less articulate will remain, of course, and will challenge the head's ingenuity in involving them in school activities and concerns. Overall, however, despite the immediate bleak financial outlook – perhaps because of it – there will be even greater expectations of primary schools.

I hope that this book, through an explanatory and

introductory approach, will offer primary headteachers some guidelines towards meeting these responsibilities. Unless the basic principles of management are appreciated, the context of decisions realised and the constraints upon actions allowed for, a headteacher will find organising his school and curriculum exacting. This is not to suggest a stultifying and rigid regime but rather a carefully planned approach which can allow for innovation and creative thought.

What I do not offer is a magical solution to complex problems. There is of course scope for the expert in planning, and in education itself, but in the end the human factor becomes paramount in both tasks. Education is about people and much of the planning for education is concerned with human resources, adult and child, professional and lay.

Day-to-day life in the primary school is carried on at a rapid pace. It is all too easy to become enclosed in the school itself, reacting only as external stimuli are applied. This is how headteachers become dictated to by events. Unfortunately it is not simple to reverse the process and shape events to the long-term needs of the school. However, a head who attempts to plan and organise his work will find it not only easier but also more rewarding.

The process of management is a means to the end of running a successful school, not an end in itself. It is a tool to be used with care. The central factor is of course the child, but occasionally one sees schools organised with everyone in mind except the pupils. The aim of the primary school manager is therefore to make the most of each child's learning opportunities and potential.

This book may raise more questions than it answers, but if that is the case I hope they will be the right questions for the head to follow up. If it succeeds in encouraging him to think in a broad way about the complex issues to be faced in running a school, and to relate those issues to the factors to be taken into account in reaching a decision, it will have been worthwhile.

1 A Job Description

Possibly the most anxious time in the career of a promotion-minded teacher is that period between the interview and the moment the chairman of the governors enters the waiting-room with the job result. The adrenalin which kept the body going during the interview itself has subsided and the waiting period has become anticlimactic. The tension is even more severe if you are applying for your first headship. Then the door opens and six hopefuls look up in anticipation: at the sound of a name one heart leaps and five drop. You have got the job.

There then follows a hectic period of congratulations, good advice, house moving and so on. But after a time a reaction often sets in: what exactly does the headteacher of a primary school do? Are you teacher or administrator? Are you public relations officer or curriculum leader? There is no easy answer to these questions and the primary head has to be a Jack of all trades. Good management will make the task easier but some idea of the work of a head is essential before you start.

As a profession, teaching has so far escaped the rigours of over-definition. Job specifications and descriptions are beginning to emerge, notably for deputy heads and heads of department in secondary schools, but often a newly appointed teacher is just shown a new class and told to get on with it; it is expected that his professionalism will see him through. The same applies to primary headteachers. Sometimes the only information you will have about your school is that it has 230 on roll, is a Group IV for salary purpose, and feeds Anytown Comprehensive. The rest of the job details consist of how much notice you must give if you get the job and dire warnings about the consequences of canvassing support.

11

This book aims to guide you along the path of good management and administration, to warn you of the many pitfalls which may upset your management, and to give you some idea of the many things which will constrain your actions. Above all it sets out to assist you in running a happy and effective primary school. What then is your real task?

First, you must accept overall responsibility for the school in the eyes of staff, children, parents, governors and the local education authority (LEA). Your line responsibility will be through the governing body to the chief education officer (CEO); it will be exercised at meetings of the governors and through your interaction with them and with LEA officers. To achieve this you must be able to communicate well, plan complicated arrangements, synthesise your actions, and treat individuals and groups in a sensitive way. In practical terms you will be expected to prepare reports for governors and possibly the LEA, and in at least one authority you will be expected to keep parents acquainted with your aims and objectives and to explain how you are achieving them.

Having accepted the responsibility for the school a headteacher must take the lead in assessing priorities and establishing favourable conditions for their achievement. School policy must be planned, therefore, with a programme of objectives to be achieved over several years. The plans will cover all aspects of the school but will essentially be invested with the resources required (space, staff, finance and equipment) to achieve the curriculum aims. You will find it necessary to keep up to date on all relevant LEA policies, and to be aware of the national consensus through the Department of Education and Science (DES) and the Schools Council.

School policies cannot be made in isolation, as will be emphasised throughout this book. Staff must be consulted, governors and parents involved, and other schools and institutions in the district taken into account. As you gain experience you may find yourself serving on relevant external committees set up by the LEA or teachers' centres. As the manager of the school you will frequently assess the curriculum and maintain a good balance between the priority of learning on the one hand and suitable enriching experiences on the other. In working closely with other headteachers, including secondary heads, and county officers and advisers, you will be expected to establish links, and to play a leading role in establishing curriculum continuity.

The control of the internal organisation and management of the school will be your responsibility and you will be expected to undertake this with a high degree of efficiency, consulting staff and senior colleagues as a matter of policy and delegating authority whenever it is reasonable to do so. A clear policy of staff development within the school should be planned, and staff experience and aptitudes must be used to establish the aims and objectives of the school, the education activities, the methodology, and to provide a regular evaluation of performance.

The activities involved in implementing this part of the job description depend very much on your own experience, personality and qualities of leadership. They include the appointment and promotion of staff, with a view to achieving immediate and longer-term objectives, and the granting of scale posts in accordance with the points allocation of the LEA. The utilisation of technology and detailed budgetary control must be set alongside the more human task of staff and pupil discipline.

It cannot be expected that a new primary headteacher will possess immediately all the skills needed to deal with these activities. Careful personal development will enable you to cope with the job but attention should be paid to gaining a grasp of basic planning methods, some of which are outlined later in this book. You should remember that your primary school is but one of many thousands in the educational system of England and Wales, and that primary education itself is only part of pre-school, secondary, tertiary and higher education provision. A detailed knowledge of your place in the system (including such particulars as Burnham) and an awareness of other social and health services will make your work more effective. You should be well aware of current curriculum developments in primary education, if only to reject them, and you should not ignore such things as the proposed common examination system at sixteen, even though it is outside your immediate terms of reference.

The job specification has so far included the management of the school, the setting and implementation of aims and objectives, and the deployment of financial and manpower resources. These can only be carried out successfully in an atmosphere of calm and trust, so a headteacher must establish good lines of communication both within the school and externally with the governors and the chief education officer. Home and school relationships are also most important.

This is a public relations function and must be seen in perspective. It does not necessarily mean inviting the local press every time the road safety officer presents cycling proficiency certificates. More important are consultations with, and visits to, local educational institutions, keeping school staff (including non-teachers) as fully informed as possible and providing an advisory service to parents and the local public. All of this demands the capacity to delegate activities and free yourself for the key tasks. Internal structures need to be organised to facilitate good communications.

Many of the points outlined above will be expanded in later sections of the book but the responsibilities mentioned have referred to general educational matters and not to the head's direct responsibility for children. This raises an important question: how far should the head be responsible for regular class teaching and how much should he restrict himself to ensuring that other members of staff carry out this responsibility?

Much depends on the size of school, the type of catchment area and its related problems, and the abilities of the staff as a whole. In most schools with fewer than 150 children the head will find himself committed to class teaching for much of the week. In larger schools the head may be the only PE or music specialist and will want to cover most of this teaching himself.

In the end it is a question of balance which you as a head must decide with regard to your own circumstances. First and foremost you are a teacher, but at the same time you are now paid to *manage* a school and all its activities. It may be very egalitarian to your colleagues to have a regular commitment in the classroom and you may feel it does your credibility good to be seen coping with the problems of teaching Fletcher or Schools Mathematics Project (SMP). But the success of your school will not be judged by the number of hours you spend in the classroom but by its overall style and well-being.

There is, of course, great danger in going to the other extreme. From time to time we have all come across the head who is never seen in the classroom. It is very important to retain close contact with primary children but this can be done in a variety of ways, from regular teaching to taking after-school activities. Above all a good head is someone who likes and interacts well with children.

Your teaching programme should be seen in the context of your job as a whole and it should be related to the time you have available. A careful analysis of this should help you in reaching that balance between the non-teaching head and the non-managing head.

The scene has been set. You are more aware of the responsibilities and tasks of headship. Now is the time to put these into the context of management.

15

2 The Nature of Management

Management and administration

The power and responsibility of the British headteacher has no parallel in the rest of the world. His position was set in the tradition of the great public school heads before education authorities assumed control of the local system. At the turn of the century central government was determined to establish a secondary education system based on existing grammar schools which confirmed the headteacher's freedom of action from the narrow constraints of local control. In turn the local authorities themselves were happy to accept the head's freedom from too much central government interference. Thus, from early in the local government system of education, the position of headteacher as a balance between various pressure groups was established; but it will be a central theme of this book that the head's freedom of action is a myth, although his power remains considerable. From this will come the view that a headteacher's responsibility to manage his school effectively and sensitively is one of his central tasks.

In the educational world concepts such as management and administration have often been thought of as rather second-rate and consequently have been relegated to an inferior position behind the teaching function. This has been particularly true of the primary school where headteachers have been offered even less in the way of management training than their secondary colleagues. Many heads proudly, and quite rightly, claim that their first love and duty is the direct teaching of the children. Bureaucratic red tape is scorned as being at best time-consuming and at worst completely irrelevant. What is often forgotten is that education, whether at national or classroom level, does not just happen but has to be carefully planned. Management should therefore be seen as indivisible from teaching; the two must complement each other if the education process is to be a success.

It is as well to be clear about definitions at the outset. There is a world of difference between administration and management, although too often the words are thoughtlessly interchanged. Administration is a much more passive task than management and does not carry the same authority. It excludes the direction of resources and, more important, it excludes policy making. The administrator makes possible what has been planned; the manager plans the policy.

One of the growth areas of further education during the past few years has been management education, but primarily in the business and industrial fields. Educational management is far more complex than its counterpart in the industrial world so it is difficult to understand why acceptance of management training for new and prospective heads has only recently been established. It may have something to do with the Englishman's love of the amateur, coupled with the perceived professional role of the teacher. Failure in industrial management can often be dramatic, as shown almost weekly by press headlines. Educational mismanagement only rarely hits the headlines, as exemplified by the William Tyndale affair. Its results, however, though less immediately tangible, can be equally devastating in their long-term consequences for both individual and the state.

Decision-making

The central importance of decison-making for the educational manager cannot be over-emphasised: the headteacher has the authority and the responsibility to take decisions which will implement his policy. This process is complicated by factors which do not always appear directly relevant. Thus, effective decisions cannot be taken without effective management.

It would be pleasant to sit down and plan from scratch, with all decision-making constrained only by our personal prejudices. A head appointed to a school still in its construction phase initially may feel that he has this opportunity. Unfortunately the new head is not often in this fortunate position as all our decisions are affected by previous ones, usually taken by other people. The head of a new school will be affected by its design and by its very location in a certain catchment area; even his freedom to choose staff to implement his own policies will be limited by the employment market at the time and the probable continuing need in the 1980s for the redeployment of teaching staff.

One vital factor in decision-making is the consideration of its long-term effects. All too often decisions are made in isolation not only of constraining factors on implementation but also of likely consequences. A headteacher may, for example, have an enthusiastic teacher taking the third year juniors who, both at college and at an LEA language centre, has undergone training in primary French. The head agrees to the introduction of French in the third year but a year later may be frustrated if he has not made plans for its continuation into the fourth year. Consequently there may be further problems for the secondary school and its other feeder primary schools. So what seemed a simple and reasonable decision affecting one teacher and perhaps thirty children has consequences far beyond its original aim.

Nor are educational planners always as aware of the possible consequences of their decision-making as they should be. Too often decisions concentrate on the narrow view and ignore the wider possibilities. All education managers must accept that today's system is the result of previous decisions, some dating back many years. In turn decisions made today will have effects not only next year but possibly into the next century. The art of decision-making is therefore not simple; it is necessary to be aware of factors acting upon the decision-maker which will affect the decision while at the same time being aware of likely future consequences. As headteachers are in the business of making decisions daily it is essential to make them carefully.

The nature of management

What do we mean by management? The word refers to the controlling process in any organisation; the managers are those who are concerned with achieving the objectives of the organisation and the use of resources to that end; in this case the resources are composed of the headteacher, his staff, capitation and other funds, equipment and, often forgotten but very important, time.

It is impossible to lay down a set of rules that an education manager can apply to all situations. In education there are no certainties although management guidelines can produce expectations and probabilities from particular courses of action. The head must manage effectively in an attempt to exclude as many of the uncertainties as possible.

Of course there are important differences between management in education and management in other walks of life and these will be detailed later. However, these differences become more evident in carrying out the non-management tasks rather than in the actual process of decision-making. The structure by which a primary head will reach a decision and follow it through will be similar to that of a chief executive or company manager; the differences will be in the constraints to be taken into account in arriving at the decision and the environment surrounding its implementation.

We can analyse the basic process of management and apply it to the school situation. A great deal has been written in this area but the main theorists would agree that the most central management elements are planning, organising, controlling and evaluating. This book is intended for the practical headteacher rather than the theorist but one must accept that sound management is more than common sense and experience. We will explore the nature of the management process a little more deeply but attempt to avoid the other extreme of accepting management as a pure science. There cannot be a set of true laws in management, therefore it cannot be a science. Management can be systematically practised but its application, particularly in the field of social provision such as education, must remain an art.

Planning

This is the basic function of management, the other functions being primarily the means through which the manager maximises his chances of making the plan a success. Planning begins with setting objectives and specifying the steps needed to attain them. The head will be concerned with the school as an institution; the head of infants will set her objectives within the overall plan, each class teacher will do the same for his class, groups or individual pupils.

Objectives can be either short-range or long-range, covering one term or the full six year primary school span. The shorter the range the more definite the plans can be and the less the risk of failure. Longer-range plans will need to be flexible to take into account changed circumstances. They also run the risk of non-completion unless definite commitments are made.

This can be illustrated by a plan to raise funds through a PTA. A project to get £200 between the summer and Christmas is attainable. The time span is reasonable with plan completion in sight acting as a motivating force. Two thousand pounds over three years may be much more difficult to achieve as there is a greater risk that interest in the project will decrease and enthusiasm decline. However, provide a terminal commitment, purchase of a swimming pool or minibus, and the chances of success are improved.

The setting of the commitment illustrates another planning problem which has been hinted at already in the discussion on decision-making. If we are not careful our view can become so narrow that we lose sight of our overall objectives. It is as well from time to time to ask ourselves the fundamental question about objectives which is: 'What business are we really in?' To do this successfully we must stand outside our immediate frame of reference and tackle the problem in a fresh manner.

This planning technique is commonly known as management by objectives, or MBO. There are many examples which could be quoted from the world of industry. IBM, one of the biggest growth industries during the sixties, defined its objectives as supplying information rather than the production of office machines. In contrast the machine tool industry lost some ground, possibly as a result of defining its task as producing metal-forming machines rather than supplying the means of production.

Attempts to define the aims and objectives of education have always run into trouble and it is not part of the present task to consider this in detail. The head must ensure, however, that he is working towards his overall objectives when he sets the purchase of a minibus or swimming pool as a commitment. It is all too easy to concentrate on a limited plan irrelevant to the main objective and thus waste valuable time while ignoring the real needs of the school.

Organisation

It is often wrongly assumed that management is mainly concerned with organisation. Without a plan to implement, even the most efficient organisation would flounder in its own bureaucracy. It is only when objectives have been defined that one can move on to a consideration of the means of building up both the material and human resources required to implement the plan.

One part of the headteacher's task is to organise his school so that the various units are not working at cross purposes or so that two units are not overlapping. How many classes have 'done' a project on the Romans two or three times during their school career without any real advancement of knowledge or skills? How often do different classes use different assessment and recording techniques?

A further problem with organisation is that of the informal group. This can be particularly relevant to the usually friendly atmosphere of the primary school without the great sub-structure of hierarchy found more commonly in the secondary school. The informal organisation consists of a network of friendships, alliances and communication channels which do not follow the usual lines. Used well the informal organisation can encourage those who are enthusiastic and make everyone feel an important part of the decision-making process. Used without thought or tact, senior members of staff will bear grudges and harbour resentment.

Control

Controlling involves translating one's plans into action through the organisation that has been built up. An important factor is the appointment of suitable staff, something which both headteachers and local authority administrators should regularly review. This is a continuing task since staff will be retiring, gaining promotion or resigning for other reasons from time to time. The fact that in a small school this may happen only once in every five years or so should not lead the head to become complacent about the appointing task; as should be self-evident the rarer and longer-term appointment in the small school can be more vital to the school as a whole than appointments in larger schools.

Controlling also means the improvement of staff through adequate training, much of which could be school-based. Heads should never become too preoccupied with day-to-day tasks so that they ignore the staff development needs of their teachers. Too often teachers choose to go on local authority courses for the wrong reasons; training courses are often made up of those who do not really need them while individuals who would benefit from some form of in-service work are ignored. Staff development and in-service education, for both individual career prospects and the needs of the school, should form a central part of the controlling task of every headteacher.

Controlling, directing or coordinating, puts together the plan and the organisation. Without a plan a happy and hard-working teaching staff could well be efficiently moving towards the wrong objective. Without organisation effective individual teachers could find their work being counteracted by others. The vital importance of control therefore becomes apparent.

Evaluation

Although evaluating education is extremely difficult it must be attempted. Whether heads like it or not they are currently open to public scrutiny under the general umbrella of accountability. It is important to ensure that those to whom we are accountable realise that education is not producing motor cars or tins of baked beans and that achievement cannot be measured in units produced per year or even on an accurate cost–benefit basis. The difficulty of achieving educational evaluation is compounded by the variable nature of the input to the system. Having said this, schools and local authorities must accept that they have a duty to monitor how well they are meeting their objectives.

Any conscious attempt to achieve some form of 'output measurement' is immediately open to cries of 'eleven-plus testing', 'payment by results' and so on. Obviously the measurement technique must remain the tool of the professional and not become his master. In any case until objectives are defined it is useless to measure achievement against them.

Because educational evaluation is difficult there is the temptation to assume that objectives can only be met or 'output' improved by increases in resources, for example, improvements in pupil–teacher ratios. A degree of indulgent and misguided spending may result on the rather dubious and unproven grounds that 'it is a good thing'. While not arguing against the case for improved resources for education, particularly in the primary school, all heads should ask what they themselves can do through better management to improve their schools.

This must be the essential task of evaluation; to allow us to appraise and improve. Evaluation must be followed by further planning otherwise management becomes a sterile exercise which ends up like so many primary school schemes of work – in the bottom drawer of the filing cabinet. The essential nature of management is that it is cyclical and not linear; management never comes to an end but is always pursuing improvements.

Why is education management different?

Although the general nature of management may be the same for the English primary school and the German steel industry there are some very distinctive features of education management which do not occur in business.

Education, unlike the business and industrial world, is not setting out to make a profit, even though the manpower theorists claim that it is an investment with a long-term return on capital. Nor are those who are engaged in the education service there to make personal fortunes. The reasons why people enter the teaching profession may vary from those who have a vocational call to those who in the words of the old saying 'teach because they cannot do'. The manager must accept that he is dealing with a group of professionally motivated people who, as a body, are both well-qualified and independent.

From this must come reinforcement of the point that education processes people and not goods. Thus the managerial relationship must be one of mutual trust and respect allowing, within flexible limits, considerable autonomy to the managed. The head's overall function must be to encourage purposeful activity without stifling individual initiative.

The difficulty of all this for the head is that, lacking clearly accepted objectives or self-evident goals, the needs of his school must be determined in a context of continuous dialogue and competing demands. These demands and the dialogue can originate from outside the teaching profession and will therefore affect his freedom of action. Many of the constraints affecting decisions are not immediately apparent to the head who in many cases still feels he retains considerable freedom of action. It is now time to consider how much of a myth is the head's so-called freedom.

3 The Myth of Autonomy

There can be few teachers who on visiting a school have not thought 'now if I were head of this school I would . . .' In making such utopian judgements we tend to forget the situational factors which might very well work against our plans, and when considering the success or lack of success of others we should bear in mind what autonomy they in fact have over their own curricula.

The pressures brought to bear upon the decision-maker in the school are both at a macro level (eg, governmental, local authority, teacher union) and at a micro level (eg, points allowances, retirement ages), but we should commence our consideration with the individual. The head who wishes to alter the curriculum of his school should consider, if he is wise, his own personality. No two heads are alike in their authority but from their personal leadership will flow the bureaucratic structure of their schools. Apart from the variety of authority taken up by heads their very effectiveness will also vary. It is therefore as well to remember that the head's autonomy can be no greater than his own quality of leadership, no matter how large or small the other pressures upon him.

Let us assume that our hypothetical head has a certain charisma enabling him to encourage and lead his fellow members of staff. This is vital if he is to achieve any curriculum changes which are to become institutionalised, as opposed to those which die a lingering death in the stockroom – but it is not enough. Many pressures, both seen and unseen, are upon him. English schools and teachers pride themselves on their degree of freedom from central governmental control. However, that freedom may be something of a myth. A head who, for instance, wished to abolish a daily assembly or regular religious instruction, would find himself breaking the law. But it is in a more subtle manner that central control usually makes itself felt.

A decision by government to promote a particular piece of legislation is very likely to force LEAs and schools to divert resources away from their top priorities. The laudable 1970 Education Act brought mentally handicapped children into the school system but its effect in some areas was to slow down the development of other parts of special education. Even more insidious perhaps are the Employment Protection Act and the Health and Safety at Work Executive. Again these are praiseworthy attempts at improving the lot of individual employees but they restrict managerial flexibility and in the case of the Health Executive may even exert a direct force on the curriculum. As another example government policy during the late seventies was to transfer central grants towards metropolitan areas and this made the task of rural authorities much more difficult. The hidden hand of government will be seen in many of the constraints which follow.

What emerges is a complex and interwoven picture of constraints on a head's autonomy. Apart from central government the macro level of constraint could be sub-divided into three main areas: resources, societal, and professional. However, these too are interlinked and can combine to restrict a head's freedom.

When considering resources, both financial and human resources must be taken into account. The local authority's ability and willingness to allow the school sufficient 'points' for adequate staff to be encouraged is important, as also is the head's flexibility in deploying his capitation allowance. It is in fact in the resource area that the local authority exerts its greatest pressure on the development of the curriculum. An LEA might have an expertise in, say, primary French, and extra money and equipment may be found for this area of the

27

curriculum, while another is relatively starved. Pressure groups within an authority, whether officers, councillors or advisers, may also influence the resources available to the school, and hence the freedom of the head in determining the curriculum. As with the other constraints the two elements of human and financial resources are entwined and this can be seen in the field of in-service training. A head who wishes to introduce family grouping will want the staff who are to undertake it to be well trained. The LEA may have funds available and be willing to set up a course; it may have funds but divert them into other areas; or it may have no spare funds whatsoever.

Of course, the converse can also be true. External factors can often influence a head into undertaking curriculum changes which are not his own decision, and in so doing may prevent him from starting a more personal scheme. Such factors may be the arrival of the local authority's adviser bearing largess if the head will undertake such and such a scheme, or the provision of a high-powered in-service course in language development which persuades the head that the county 'believes in' language development, and therefore if the head introduces it he will do his promotion prospects no harm.

I have concentrated on resources as applied to in-service training, but a local authority can encourage or restrict the curriculum through the manipulation of resources in other areas. If the county architect builds new primary schools on an open plan basis then a curriculum suited to such schools will be encouraged. If a museum loan service operates it will help those heads who wish to encourage lively history teaching. Many other examples can be cited showing how authorities can encourage development in one field but restrict it in another.

The methods open to a head of influencing the decisions of an LEA in the resource area are limited. If he is fortunate he may be nominated as a representative member of the education committee and thereby gain a voice in direct decision-making. More possibly he may sit on a variety of working parties, the decisions of which influence the curriculum in his own school. Even more likely still, he may, as a member of a professional association, become part of a pressure group which has varying degrees of success. But it must be accepted that a head has more control over the constraints peculiar to his own school, than over a county-wide area.

Despite what some teachers might think, schools are provided for the benefit of society as a whole and not just to give employment to a work force of half a million. It is perhaps reasonable that society should exert some pressure on curriculum decisions, and this is done in both an overt and a covert way.

The labour market, as the employing section of the community, exerts a very real influence on the decisions of the headteacher. In general terms the employers' demands for certificates of competence have encouraged the extension of the examination system from GCE to CSE and now to CEE. The examinations themselves restrict considerably the options open for curriculum development in the upper secondary school, even with the introduction of Mode 3.

If the expectations of employers restrict options nationally, the very existence (or lack of it) of local industry can have a dramatic effect on individual schools. A head wishing to introduce business courses in a rural community is likely to encounter opposition as might the head of an East London comprehensive in attempting to introduce rural studies. The latter head may have excellent educational, even social, reasons for showing the children of Stepney that milk does not come from a bottle, but the relevance of such a course is bound to be questioned by the local community. Although the influence of examinations and employers is felt more directly by secondary schools, primary heads should not ignore completely their indirect and perhaps hidden influence on the primary curriculum.

The community may be concerned at a lack of literacy or

numeracy in schools, and political capital can easily be made from this, developing the concern still further. In such a climate the headteacher might well think twice before introducing some aspect of the curriculum which might seem to trivialise 'real' learning. The impact and follow-up of Prime Minister Callaghan's 'Ruskin' speech at Oxford in 1976 is likely to be with us for some time. Communities are no more homogeneous than headteachers and thus the constraints of one area may be the enthusiasm of the next. The primary head wishing to start sex education may find great difficulty in persuading parents to agree to it while a neighbouring school is operating such a scheme very successfully.

Apart from numerous informal contacts with the community at large the head is likely to meet 'society' in two formal ways: through a parent–teacher association (PTA) or some other association of parents, if one exists at his school, and at meetings of governors or managers. The PTA will provide the more articulate parents with a platform to voice their opinions on the curriculum, but at the same time will allow the head to display his curriculum wares to advantage. How many schools have held parents' evenings on 'Nuffield Maths'? A head can also use a PTA to encourage certain schemes positively by raising money for a kiln, or infant equipment, or a video-tape machine.

If heads are able to control PTAs more easily than they can the LEA, the same might also be said for the head's relationship with his governors. In theory at least the governors have responsibility for the curriculum, and a wise head can use his governors to get that little extra from resources which will turn his innovation into action.

Of very great importance to the head as a decision-maker will be the professional opinion of his colleagues outside the school. Closest to hand will be the heads of neighbouring schools and the sensible head will work closely with them on curriculum innovation. He will steer clear of projects which will make transfer across the board or up the ladder difficult: an infant head should consult junior colleagues before introducing new reading methods and a tertiary principal would be unwise to demand British Constitution as a course entrance requirement if it is not taught in the feeder secondaries.

The influence of advisers will make itself felt and they can act as encouragers or dampeners of enthusiasm. As they often have small funds of their own they can influence the curriculum beyond the credibility of their own reputation.

Professional advisory bodies such as the Schools Council and the Council for Education Technology will also restrict the autonomy of the head, if only to suggest ideas which the head later regards as his own. A consensus of a sensible or relevant curriculum is handed down from such bodies and heads will think very carefully before going against such ideas. Professional acceptance is a weighty thing for the decision-maker to have on his side.

We have seen so far how many constraints conspire together to restrict the autonomy of the head. Take the simple example of a new reading scheme which a school wishes to introduce: there may not be enough money to buy it; there may not be teachers trained to use it effectively; the advisers may not like it; parents might not consider it relevant; the Schools Council may not give it their imprimatur. At the same time we must realise that education is a business and a head must be very strong to resist the pressures of all these groups if they are urging him to take up a particular scheme.

But let us assume that our head has gained the necessary resources, has convinced the parents and is in accordance with accepted educational opinion. He is all set to go: or is he? It is at this stage that he has to face the internal, micro factors which restrict his autonomous action. Unless the head is fortunate enough to have been consulted frequently on the design of his school, and to have chosen his complete staff, any changes he might make will have to be within an inherited framework.

The size of school and the buildings, the determinants of which lie largely outside the head's prerogative, can profoundly influence decision-making within the school. The very size of the establishment can limit the available number of allowances above Scale 1 and this affects the options open to the innovator. The architecture of the school strongly influences curricular decisions. A modern open-plan primary school will encourage cooperative teaching: a century-old school will make a different learning situation inevitable.

While both the size and shape of the school influence internal decision-making, just as important is its situation. A neighbourhood school in an urban area cannot sustain all the activities of a rural school. The local authority zoning system will determine the type of child who comes to the school, and hence the curriculum which is suitable.

When attempting to change curricula the head must be aware of the existing curriculum. Reading schemes in primary schools cannot be changed overnight; maths courses cannot be altered in mid-stream. If new concepts are to be accepted and made to work the head must bide his time.

A headteacher can manipulate to his advantage some buildings and he can also adjust his staffing and organisational structure to suit his own ideas, within the confines already suggested. However, if he fails to carry the teaching staff with him it is certain that his changes will fail. The experience of the teachers in working with the new methods, their personalities, their willingness to work as a team, will all contribute to the success or failure of new schemes. A wise head can convince his staff to alter their existing arrangements, but he will lead rather than force. He must be aware that some staff, perhaps as able and dedicated as himself, may themselves wish to make changes which conflict with his own views. Various groups may well form within a staff and need delicate handling. It may be a truism, but any curriculum development will only be as good as the teaching staff.

It is clear that the head's freedom to choose his curriculum is circumscribed, right from the type of pupil before him up to the Secretary of State. A head who is aware of these constraints will be able to manipulate the system and make compromises with every chance of success. A head who attacks the problem directly may well decide never to become involved in controversial decision-making again. It is now appropriate to look in more detail at the primary school and its headteacher in relation to these constraints.

4 Education Management in Central and Local Government

Any primary teacher who has worked in more than one local authority will know that the experience of education can vary to quite a large degree from one place to another. This is the result of power and authority in education residing among a number of people and organisations, especially headteachers, local authorities, the Department of Education and Science, and Parliament. Teachers, but even more so parents, find it difficult to know who to turn to for decisions, advice and appeals. The aim of this chapter is to show who is responsible for what, and where the primary head fits into the scheme of things.

The Department of Education and Science

The political chief of the DES is the Secretary of State, a senior member of the government with a seat in the cabinet. He is responsible for all functions of the education service in England as well as other aspects of the arts and science. Welsh schools are administered from the Welsh Office by the Secretary of State for Wales.

The administrative head of the DES is the Permanent Under-Secretary of State who, as his title suggests, is likely to be at the department longer than his minister. Departments within the DES deal with specific branches of the service and territorial teams deal with matters relating to the LEAs in their area.

The ears and eyes of the DES are, of course, Her Majesty's Inspectors, headed by a senior chief inspector. However, HMIs are jealous of their independence which is symbolised in their title and in their formal appointment by the monarch. About forty HMIs work at Elizabeth House, headquarters of the DES, and a few are seconded to other organisations such as the Schools Council or are posted abroad. The majority will be assigned to territorial divisions covering part of the country.

HMIs have as a basic function the advice and inspection of schools and in doing this they disseminate knowledge about curriculum and organisation. This is backed up by the many long and short courses organised by the inspectorate. They also meet regularly with LEA officers to act as an important, but not the sole, means of communication between the LEA and the DES.

Increasingly since Prime Minister Callaghan's speech at Ruskin College, Oxford, which started the 1977 great debate on education, the inspectorate has spent time on centrally based activities such as the 1978 survey of primary schools, and contributing to the growing collection of occasional papers on aspects of the education service. It is also involved with departmental working parties and other committees such as the National Foundation for Educational Research (NFER), Council for National Academic Awards (CNAA) and the Schools Council.

The 1944 Education Act instructs the Secretary of State 'to promote the education of people' and 'to secure the effective execution by local authorities, under his control and direction, of the national policy for providing a varied and comprehensive education service in every area'. But the DES does not build schools, it does not employ teachers and, despite ventures into the curriculum in the late seventies, it does not prescribe what should be taught.

In reality the Secretary of State has a regulating function, setting down minimum standards of provision and the context in which the service must be administered locally. He achieves this through the control of resources and through regulation. Resources are controlled via finance, buildings and teachers, and these are discussed in detail in other chapters of the book. It is worth spending a little time here considering the control of LEAs through regulations.

Regulations

ACTS OF PARLIAMENT

It is through Parliament that all legislation must pass and since, in the end, our education is dependent on the law it is in Parliament that the ultimate control resides. Our present system is based upon the 1944 Education Act, amended and extended by a number of less comprehensive acts since. These acts determine what should happen by making it somebody's specific responsibility. Duties are imposed upon individuals or institutions and they are given the power to carry them out. In many cases there is an element of discretion between the duty of an authority and its power. Both central and local government are told what they must do, or may do, through the various acts; any action beyond this would be *ultra vires*, that is, beyond the law. This could include, for example, any LEA attempting to prescribe what mathematics books could be used in its schools.

STATUTORY INSTRUMENTS

These are issued by the DES and have the force of law. They normally detail the conditions necessary to adhere to a general clause in an Act of Parliament. The 1944 Act says education must be full-time for school children; the 1959 Regulation or Statutory Instrument details how many days and hours this in fact means.

CIRCULARS

These set out in detail the government's policy on particular

36

issues. Many of them are in fact non-party political, dealing with such things as school meals. However, the more well-known tend to be controversial, such as 10/65 on comprehensive reorganisation. The second set of figures on a circular identify the year in which it was issued.

ADMINISTRATIVE MEMORANDA

These give advice to authorities on specific topics, usually interpretation of Education Acts.

The DES has in the past had a reputation for being isolationist, cut off from the rest of government thinking. This may have been partly because ministers and civil servants became almost totally involved in the educational world. We are now seeing a change of emphasis away from this detached view of education towards one of greater accountability and involvement in curriculum issues. Initiatives started under the Labour government of 1974–9 include the setting up of the Assessment of Performance Unit and the so called 'Great Debate'. The latter involved wide-ranging discussions on the curriculum at a series of conferences and set every LEA the task of completing a list of questions sent out in a DES circular. The department is, of course, still restricted to its role within legislative limits but it is now taking a stronger lead in collecting and disseminating examples of good practices. The role of central government is, therefore, being sharpened although, as we shall see, the local authorities, teacher associations and schools will not easily be subordinated to central control, particularly since many HMIs are reluctant to go too far along the centralist road.

Local education authorities

The 1944 Act says in section 6 that: 'the local education authority for each county shall be the council of the county, and the local education authority of each county borough shall be

37

the council of the county borough.' These councils derived their powers from the County Councils Act of 1888 and the Education Act of 1902, but a major change took place in 1965 when the Greater London Council took over the administration of Middlesex and parts of Kent, Essex, Hertfordshire and Surrey. The Outer London Boroughs were given responsiblity for education but within the boundary of the new London County Council a special elected education authority was set up known as the Inner London Education Authority (ILEA).

The rest of England and Wales was reorganised in 1974. A Royal Commission set out the basic principles to be followed which were: that local authority areas should have a common purpose based on the interdependence of town and country; that the responsibility for personal services should be with the same authority (eg, education, social services); that the new authorities should be normally larger than the old county boroughs, yet small enough to remain in touch with the public.

As a result of this the number of LEAs was reduced in 1974 from 163 to 104. The new local government system is basically two-tier with county and district councils. In metropolitan areas the district is responsible for education, in the remainder it is the responsibility of the county. Reorganisation had a profound effect on many parts of the country: proud county boroughs became parts of a shire county and lost their educational independence; new counties such as Avon tried to consolidate the educational provision made previously by four authorities (Somerset, Gloucestershire, Bristol and Bath); a few counties disappeared or became rumps of their former selves, eg, Somerset.

At the same time reorganisation took place in the Health Service, and Area Health Authorities (AHA) took over many of the responsibilities of the School Health Service previously exercised by local authorities. Understandably the AHAs were based on hospital provision but this has caused boundary problems in some parts of the country. A quarter of the

Somerset LEA is administered by the Wiltshire AHA with consequent problems of coordination and liaison.

All is not well with these reorganisations, although it should be said that they have had only a few years to prove themselves during a time of rapid inflation and scarce resources. However, another health service reorganisation is quite likely and the ten major cities in the country may eventually gain control of some personal services, possibly including education, as a result of so-called 'organic change'.

MEMBERS

In the main there are three groups of people who work in the administration of a local education authority: elected members, officers and advisers or inspectors. It is the elected members, the councillors, who are ultimately responsible for the decisions of the local education authority, and they are elected by us, the public, at the regular local elections.

It is important for the headteacher to remember that a council has other functions beyond education, and members of the council may have other interests beyond education, or indeed no interest in education at all. However, before deciding on any educational matter a council must consider a report from its education committee to which it may delegate any educational functions apart from the levying of a rate.

The education committee will have a majority of elected laymen, but it will be augmented by co-opted members who must have experience in education or be acquainted with the educational conditions in the area. The education committee will set up a number of sub-committees charged with specific tasks or the overseeing of specific areas of policy or management. The structure of sub-committees varies from one authority to another but a typical example is shown in the diagram overleaf.

The schools sub-committee will consider policy relating to the statutory parts of the school system and in some authorities there are separate primary and secondary committees. 'Schools sub' tends to be prestigious and there can be a heavy work-load for members. The further education (FE) sub-committee is concerned with post-school education and may cover youth and adult education, although these areas are sometimes separate committees or combined into a community sub-committee. Local education authorities are among the largest estate managers in the country and the buildings sub-committee will be involved in all aspects of site purchase and disposal, as well as liaising with schools and FE sub over building programmes. The special services sub-committee will have responsibility for the education of handicapped children and it is likely that the recommendations of the Warnock Report will cause some changes in the make-up and responsibilities of this committee. Frequently special services will also encompass more general services such as transport, school meals and crossing patrol duties. Finally, some authorities have an executive committee known as chairman's sub-committee which allows sub-committee chairmen to discuss issues of a broad policy nature before meetings of the full education committee.

The committee structure may appear cumbersome even though there have been some attempts at streamlining since reorganisation in 1974. It does enable the more important policy issues to be discussed in detail several times before the policy is confirmed by full council although urgent matters can be undertaken by the chairman through 'chairman's action', and reported at the next sub-committee meeting, or by officers under delegated powers.

Matters of detail or policy will go before the appropriate sub-committee and any decisions will be recommended in a report to the full education committee. Here any decisions can be questioned and if the full committee is not satisfied the matter can be referred back to the sub-committee for further discussion. If expenditure is involved the decision may be passed to a finance committee (comprising members who may be apathetic to, or even anti-education, as well as the pro-education lobby) and then to full council. In some authorities the finance committee, or the policy and resources committee, acts as a type of Cabinet, but it must be remembered that before any council, in its capacity as the local education authority, takes a decision on any education matter, it must by law ask for a report from its education committee.

OFFICERS

It is the elected members of the council who carry the ultimate responsibility for the LEA's service but they delegate the day-to-day administration to, and are advised by, professional education officers. The professional staff are headed by a chief education officer and he is assisted by a number of officers with specific responsibilities, usually relating to sub-committee areas. In many parts of the country the education service is the biggest local enterprise, with an annual budget, even in a small area, of £80 million, and therefore the task of the education officer is similar to that of a manager in a large company. Even third tier officers, only a few years from their last teaching post, can find themselves responsible for budgets of £10 million or more. Education officers are recruited from qualified, honours graduate teachers and have their own professional association, the Society of Education Officers, and their own trade union, the Association of Education Officers.

Just as the sub-committee structure varies from one authority to another so does the education officer hierarchy and indeed the nomenclature. However, a typical structure is:

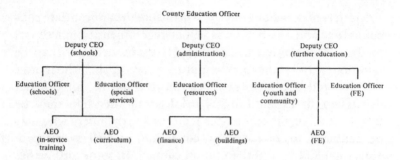

In recent years an increasing number of CEOs have moved towards a multiple deputy arrangement, with each deputy taking charge of a branch of the service; this is a more effective means of management than having a line deputy.

The professional education officers, recruited from a teaching background, are supported by administrative and clerical staff, the more senior of whom will have graduate, or graduate equivalent, qualifications in management or administration. The services of the treasurer and the architect will usually be shared with the rest of the authority.

The precise relationships between elected member and education officer will vary with the structure of the authority, the political make-up and motivation of the majority party, and the individual character and personality of chief officer and chairman of committee. Generally the members will agree the policy, officers will implement it. The policy may often be decided on the basis of a report from the CEO but the officers are not the sole repositories of policy ideas. In essence the officer represents the 'educational' constituency based on a knowledge of, and expertise in, the teaching profession. The member represents the wider needs of the community and if a primary head wishes to fight a policy decision he must direct his criticisms to member as well as to officer.

ADVISERS

Each LEA will have a larger or smaller force of educational

advisers with a dual, and sometimes conflicting, role. The adviser's job is to support and advise individual schools and heads, and also to advise the chief education officer on specific parts of his service. In doing this he may take on some degree of an inspectorial function. In 1968 Sir W. Houghton identified seven major tasks of a local adviser:

1 help with staff requirements and promotion;
2 encouragement and help to young teachers;
3 development of in-service and induction training;
4 transmission of current educational thinking;
5 advice on new buildings and equipment;
6 appraisal of individual schools as a whole;
7 channel of communication between school and administration.

The HMI has a brief to ensure that local educational standards are adequate, and to monitor the nation's provision as a whole. The local adviser will be concerned to gain sufficient resources for his own subject for the schools in his area and to make certain that their needs are presented at 'court'. A head can seek the support of an adviser for his particular requirements but he should not forget that the adviser also has a duty to make sure that LEA policies are being carried out.

Local advisers may have an area, or pastoral function; they may have a specialist function, such as mathematics, language development or music; or they may have a phase function, such as primary, infant or special. They will usually report to the chief education officer via a chief adviser, and they may have the support of a number of advisory teachers whose job will entail more direct work within the classroom, often of an in-service training nature.

If a primary head is to manage his school effectively he needs to know his key advisers. Contrary to popular mythology most advisers are not refugees from the classroom. They have held senior positions in schools at head of department or headship level, and their acquaintance with a large number of schools enables them to offer fair and objective support. The advisory service offers a head the opportunity to make the most of his resources, human and financial, and it offers him an entrée to the decision-making world of the authority.

Pressure Groups

An increasing influence on the decision-making processes of our modern democracy has been exerted by the various pressure groups representing the collective and sometimes sectionalised interest of their members. It is possible to distinguish between those groups which are accepted as an almost formal part of the policy machinery bureaucracy and those which operate outside the system but with sometimes surprisingly effective results. Examples of the latter are the teachers' campaign against corporal punishment (STOPP) and the National Federation of Parent Teacher Associations.

Although the informal groups may well cause headaches for a headteacher from time to time, or although he may in fact be a member of one of them, the longer-term effects of the pressure groups' action will come from those that are accepted as part of the consultative process. These groups fall into two main sections: those which act as the collective voice of the local authority employers, and those which act for the teachers. A third section which may well have an increasing influence on headteachers and the management of education generally comprise other public sector unions, notably the National Association of Local Government Officers (NALGO) and the National Union of Public Employees (NUPE). At this stage we are more concerned with teachers and employers.

Until 1973 there were six local authority associations covering England and Wales including the Association of Education Committees (AEC). The AEC, under the energetic leadership of Lord Alexander, kept the influence of education high within the local authority structure but soon after the reorganisation of local government in 1974 the new authorities claimed that lcoal government educational interests should represent education *authorities* and not education committees. With fewer committees continuing in membership the AEC was forced to disband and the most dominant voice on the education scene since the war went into well-earned retirement.

This meant that after reorganisation three national groups represented local authorities and one of these (the Association of District Councils) was not involved in education. The other two remain – the Association of County Councils (ACC) and the Association of Metropolitan Authorities (AMA) covering metropolitan counties, metropolitan districts, the GLC, the London Boroughs and the City of London. The AMA and the ACC have set up their own joint educational organisation, the Central Council of Local Education Authorities (CLEA).

The local authority associations have a continuing dialogue with government and are formally consulted on legislation, circulars and other issues of relevance to local education authorities. They have a statutory right to be involved in the determination of the rate support grant (RSG) and of teachers' salaries. Their evidence is sought on every committee affecting education and they have members on all educational councils and consultative committees. They also have a close relationship with a significant number of MPs. Therefore, when you vote in your local elections your vote not only goes to determine the eventual policy of your own education authority, but also, by extension, wields an influence on the national scene.

The teachers' unions would not see themselves as part of the establishment but they are perhaps more involved than they recognise. They cannot work from the same base as other trade unions because they represent among their membership headteachers who manage the institutions which collectively form the establishment. They also represent rank and file teachers who are concerned with working in a system which is part of the establishment. Their day-to-day negotiations are with education officers most of whom are teachers themselves and some of whom may still be 'left profession' members of the union. Furthermore, the broad membership of the unions makes it difficult to get agreement except on fairly wide issues such as working conditions and salaries. Despite some industrial action in the seventies and a more militant stance on individual issues the teacher unions remain essentially soft in their relationships with government and basically conservative in outlook.

However, the unions are powerful bodies with a joint membership of around half a million. In consultative status they are very close to the local authority associations and they are consulted about most of the issues which affect the interest of their members or educational policy in general. At local level a Teachers Consultative Committee, comprising LEA members and representatives of the recognised teacher unions, will offer advice and comment to the education committee. The unions have a dual function: to act in a usual trade union role by advancing the conditions of their members (and making the assumption that what is good for teachers is good for education as a whole) and to act as a force in creating opinion about the organisation and content of education.

As is the case with most union–employer relations the differences get far more publicity than the agreements. The unions have frequent meetings with local officials and on many issues the local authority will share the union view rather than the view of the DES. On some of these issues education officers will identify with the teachers' interests. And where differences remain, there is at least a shared understanding of the problem involved.

In the last fifteen years the influence and behaviour of the teachers' unions has broadened. As government has become more involved in the economic functioning of the country through such means as pay and prices policies, the teachers' unions have sought an entrée to the powerful economic departments of government. This has led to the National Union of Teachers (NUT), the National Association of Schoolmasters/Union of Women Teachers (NAS/UWT) and the former Association of Teachers in Technical Institutions (ATTI) becoming full and active members of the TUC. At the same time teachers have found themselves, with doctors and nurses, as part of a more financially aware group of vocationally oriented professionals, as they see economic and social values changing around them.

Government in education is, therefore, a complex business and the unwary head can be caught out by the confusing and sometimes ambiguous nature of the relationships. The sensible head will be aware of the constraints upon him through the central and local government system but he will also know how to use the system through its checks and balances and through its formal and informal set up to bring his own influence to bear.

5 School Governors

School governors, or managers as those in primary schools used to be known, are a tier of educational administration peculiar to England and Wales. No similar body exists in the rest of the world and their presence reflects the evolution of English education which has combined community and political involvement with the devolution of as much power as possible to local level.

County schools

Maintained schools comprise all schools run by local education authorities and this sector includes both county and voluntary schools. The whole cost of running a maintained school is met by the LEA and this includes maintenance of all the fabric in the case of county schools. At the moment two-thirds of the governors are appointed by the LEA and one-third by the minor authority ('the Council of any borough, or district or rural parish in the area served by the school and where the school serves more than one area then all these minor authorities acting jointly'). In a county school religious education and worship must be undenominational and in accordance with the agreed syllabus.

Aided schools

An aided school is a voluntary school provided by a religious denomination or an educational trust. The governors must be able and willing to find 15 per cent of the cost of any enlargement or improvement to bring the school up to

48

regulation standards. Two-thirds of the governors are called foundation managers, appointed by the body controlling the school and having a particular duty to ensure that the school is run in accordance with the trust deed.

Religious education is controlled by the governors and must be in accordance with the trust deed. Secular instruction remains under the control of the local education authority.

Teachers are appointed by the governors and remain their 'servants', subject to the establishment set by the LEA and the authority's acceptance of their ability and qualifications to teach secular subjects. School meals staff are appointed by the LEA, but non-teaching staff, subject to the authority's requirements, are appointed by governors.

The governors are responsible for the exterior maintenance and repair of the building, with an 85 per cent contribution from the DES. The LEA is responsible for the interior.

Controlled schools

These are voluntary schools where the governors have surrendered their responsibility for finding 15 per cent of the cost of improving or enlarging the school. This has passed to the LEA who accept the whole cost of such improvements. In return the LEA controls the appointment of teachers, although the governors must be involved in the appointment of the head and the authority must agree to a percentage of the teaching staff being 'reserved teachers' for religious education. This must be in accordance with the agreed syllabus but denominational instruction may be provided twice a week.

The instrument of government

This defines the membership and contribution of governing bodies and although instruments vary they generally include the provisions shown overleaf.

1 The constitution and the appointment of any *ex officio* member (ie, the parish incumbent).
2 The tenure of appointment of members, generally speaking for the life of the local education authority, although foundation governors often have a life of five years.
3 Method of appointing the chairman and vice-chairman (unless stated in the instrument the incumbent is not *ex officio* chairman in a voluntary school).
4 Provision for preventing the appointment of governors having a financial interest in the school.
5 Arrangements to end the tenure of a member for bankruptcy, incapacity or resignation, and to fill such casual vacancies.
6 Provision for calling and recording meetings, and their frequency.

Usually the instrument for county schools is a general one; each voluntary school has its own.

Articles of government

Again these vary from place to place but they are designed to guide governors and heads in the management of schools. Their central purpose is to define the function of the governors and set limits to the authority and relationship of governors *vis-à-vis* the head and the LEA. The articles will normally include:

1 the place of the school in the educational system;
2 the general conduct of the school, ie, in accordance with provisions of Parliament, the articles of government and the LEA regulations;
3 the financial responsibilities of governors. This is generally limited to having general financial oversight in the case of primary schools although most governors are able to authorise minor repairs. Governors usually happily accept their task of informing the LEA when, in their belief, financial resources have failed to meet the school's needs.

Some authorities are devolving more financial responsibility to schools and in these areas the governors' role will be enhanced;

4 the upkeep of premises, including the carrying out of minor repairs, informing the LEA of the needs of the school for changes in accommodation, and the use of school premises outside school hours subject to the provision of the LEA and the Education Acts;

5 the appointment, suspension or dismissal of non-teaching staff;

6 the organisation of the school, including conduct and curriculum;

7 the fixing of occasional holidays;

8 dealing with leave of absence requests from staff, subject to the LEA's regulations;

9 the suspension of pupils.

Provision is made for full consultation between the head, governors and local education authority and opportunity is given for assistant staff to make their views known either through the head or in some cases by attendance at the meeting. Heads are entitled to attend governors' meetings unless excluded for good reason during the discussion of specific business.

Copies of the articles must be given to every teacher upon appointment, or facilities made available to them for reading the articles. Few teachers take up the opportunity to read them but the advice to all new heads is, read and understand your articles of government.

The Education Bill, 1978

In April 1975 the government set up a Committee of Inquiry under Councillor Tom Taylor to 'review the arrangements for the management and government of maintained primary and secondary schools in England and Wales, including the composition and function of bodies of managers and governors, and their relationships with local education authorities, with new teachers and staff of schools, with parents of pupils and the local community at large; and to make recommendations.'

The committee reported in 1977 under the title, 'A New Partnership for our Schools' and the recommendations included a four-way governing body of LEA representatives, school staff, parents (and where appropriate pupils) and the local community. Minor authority representation would be abolished and the headteacher would be an *ex officio* governor. The new Taylor governors would set the aims of the school and review progress towards meeting these aims. Systematic training for governors was also recommended.

Reaction to the Taylor proposals was swift. Some authorities claimed that they were already meeting many of the recommendations; a survey in 1979 showed that most authorities already made provision for parent and teacher governors. The minor authorities naturally resented losing their direct representation and most headteachers felt their position as an adviser to the governors was stronger than being an *ex officio* member. In the area of the 'secret garden of the curriculum' one teachers' leader claimed that the proposals were 'a busybodies' charter'. One of the strongest arguments against Taylor was the cost of the proposals: one authority estimated a doubling of administrative costs attributable to 'Taylor' governors.

After due consultation the Secretary of State introduced a bill into the 1978 session of Parliament which included sections on the government of schools. The main features of the bill relating to governing bodies were:

1 All primary schools were to have 'governors' in place of managers (throughout this book the term 'governor' has been used).

2 The Secretary of State was to be enabled by regulations to determine the composition and size of all governing bodies but would be required to ensure that they included:
(a) those appointed by the local education authority;
(b) those who are teachers in the school (elected by the teachers);
(c) those who are parents of children in the school (elected by the parents);
(d) representatives of the community in the case of secondary schools.
The sections of the 1944 Act dealing with the prescriptions on the composition of governing bodies were due for repeal. The White Paper published after the bill outlined the regulations by which 2 would have been achieved and they were far more flexible than the original Taylor proposals.
3 Elections for teachers and parents were to be under rules made by the Secretary of State.
4 Provision for voluntary schools to be included in the general arrangements with the current one-third proportions being changed.

The fall of the Labour government in March 1979 meant that the bill was lost in the 1978–9 session of Parliament. However, the Conservative government elected in May 1979 promised legislation in due course to safeguard parental rights and reform school governing bodies.

Working with governors

Some heads are afraid to make a decision without the consent of their governors while others hold governors in contempt. The wise run their own ship but enter into a partnership with governors and keep them fully informed. If governors are expected to play a central and active part in the life of the school, and to discuss, although not control, professional as well as procedural matters, a partnership of benefit to both parties can be established.

It can be very frustrating to explain educational matters to a committee of laymen, but it can bring the head back to earth. If the governors cannot understand the head's policies, are they good policies? Used well a governing body can be a great source of strength for the head, especially in his relations with County Hall. Used badly splits will develop, which in a small village community can have catastrophic results.

The key governor is the chairman, so arrange to meet him fairly regularly between meetings. Ask his advice on community matters and show him the work of the school. Invite all the governors to make regular visits to the school; indeed it is fair to tell them that you expect them to show such an interest. Ask the governors to invite members of your staff to occasional meetings so that they can explain the work of their classes or the area of the curriculum for which they have responsibility.

If governors are to feel part of the school they should be known well both by staff and by parents. If they are prepared to work hard and conscientiously, and if you as head are prepared to work with them, they will be a source of encouragement and assistance in what can often be a lonely job.

6 Primary School Finance

Heads of primary schools, particularly the smaller ones, often feel themselves to be the Cinderellas of the education service. The source of much of this feeling can be traced back to the apparent inadequate funding of primary education. Although the head's major and immediate problems may be the stretching of his capitation allowance it is worth reflecting on where the primary school fits into the set-up of education and the economy. If the headteacher can understand how the budget is compiled he has taken a major step in recognising his financial responsibility.

Education is by far the most expensive local government service and this can cause jealousy from other services and make it the first target of the treasurer's department in any cutbacks. It is not just the size of the education budget which causes comment but also its rapid growth. Although the comparison of statistics is always open to question (and there is not even agreement over what contributes education in total) it is clear that the service now has a much larger share of national resources than it did at the beginning of the century.

One reason for this is the increase of pupil numbers due to bulges in the birthrate, the raising of the school leaving age (ROSLA), better take-up rates in further education and so on. Many local politicians and economists would argue that the present dramatic decline in the birthrate should lead to a lessening of the demand for resources but as we shall see later the reverse is just the case; educationalists argue that not only does a slump in the birthrate give us an opportunity to improve matters but, *pro rata*, more must be pumped into the system merely for it to stand still.

55

Other reasons contributing to increased educational expenditure are the general growth of the economy as a whole, and major policy changes. It is in these areas that primary schools appear to have suffered relative to secondary, further and even special education. As an economy expands so does the demand for skilled manpower but it is to the secondary sector that resources are sent to meet the demand. The education acts of this century have been concerned with expansion at the upper end of schooling and resource allocation has reflected this. Secondary reorganisation and ROSLA have both been looked at enviously by primary heads, at least in terms of resource provision. On the other hand it seems that recent cuts have relatively improved the position of primary education.

When headteachers complain about the inadequacy of primary staffing ratios or capitation allowances they are often bewildered by the range of reasons given by the LEA. Building allocations, RSG, Public Expenditure Surveys, the Pool (see p. 62), and so on, seem to put up a smoke screen beyond which it is difficult to see.

Capital

There are, first of all, two major financial budgets of local councils – capital and revenue. Capital expenditure goes on the building and remodelling of schools. Each LEA submits to the DES a bid for a building allocation and is then notified before the beginning of the financial year how much it has been allocated. The DES allocation is in fact only permission for the LEA to spend its own money; it is not, as is often thought, an actual cash grant to the authority. The government uses these allocations as one way of regulating the national economy. After an authority has been notified of its allocation it will decide which projects can go forward and it will then set about borrowing the money required, usually through the Local Government Loan Board.

Revenue

Revenue is quite separate from capital and is the money which is used each year to cope with running costs. This expenditure includes the salaries of all employees, including teachers, capitation allowances, maintenance of school premises, in-service education, school meals, school transport and so on. Salaries and wages form the major part of the LEA's expenditure with teachers' salaries taking nearly 50 per cent of the total. In such a labour-intensive business this is not surprising although in recent years the proportion of teachers' salaries to non-teachers' has altered in the latter's favour. Now nearly 50 per cent of the people employed by an LEA are non-teachers and this has caused some criticism of an over-bureaucratic service. In fact the majority of these people are welfare assistants, clerical assistants in schools, school meals staff, cleaners and so on. All of these services are provided by the local authority but if we look not just at how the money is spent but also at where it comes from we shall see that central government plays a substantial part.

The budget

The budget-making process of any LEA is a very complicated business starting many months and often years before the beginning of the financial year. Estimates have to be made about the cost of continuing existing policies, allowing for different pupil numbers and any changes in the number of days a school is open during the year. Budgets for development items such as improved pupil–teacher ratios will be prepared in the hope that sufficient resources will be available to implement them. The budget then has to be prepared alongside the resources likely to be available and political decisions may have to be taken between raising the rate or contracting the service. But where do the resources come from?

Rates

The basic source of local authority income is the rate, although it is not the largest source. There has been much criticism in recent years about the inequitable system of levying rates and changes are likely in the not too distant future. However, the final result will be similar – money will be raised locally for local purposes.

Many people judge how well or badly a council is doing by the size of the rate demand each May. While most constituents are prepared for a modest 1 per cent or 2 per cent rise to improve services they have been horrified at the large increases of 15–20 per cent during the last few years due almost entirely to inflation. Council members are, therefore, very cautious about approving additional rate increases even when they are told that 100 extra teachers could be employed for just an extra penny on the rates.

There are other problems in justifying rate increases for education. What is a trifling sum in the education budget could make a major improvement in other services and, therefore, non-education committee members are likely to be sceptical of education's claims. Furthermore, there is little tangible evidence of 'value for money' in education as the service is one of the most difficult to quantify. Even if reasonable measuring tools could be agreed the results could not be seen in the short term. Council members have to rely in a large part, therefore, on the professional expertise and prejudice of teachers and education officers.

On the other hand, education has had, at least until recently, an emotional pull, and tends to be a good vote catcher. Education costs themselves are rarely criticised by the public although the distribution of resources within the service might be. There does now seem to be a trend, however, towards greater financial accountability, accentuated no doubt by the difficult financial situation generally, the sheer size of the education budget, and the inability of education to be the cure for all the social and economic ills we were told it would be in the sixties.

Education policy, whether the primary head likes it or not, has to be considered in the light of resources. As the revenue from rates has at least the virtue of some flexibility the limiting factor is not so much any proposed new policy itself but the political advisability of rate increases. Unfortunately, as we have seen, education is labour intensive. This, when added to the mandatory nature of much educational expenditure, means that anything other than basic provision is at risk. However, it is in these 'at risk' areas where educational progress can best be achieved.

Local authorities have not been able to raise enough from the rates even to cover basic services, however, and the bulk of the difference is provided by the government under a very complicated formula.

Rate support grant

The system of the rate support grant is meant to supplement the cash which an authority receives from the rates. RSG was introduced in 1966 as a refinement of the general grant which had been paid since 1958. The grant covers all services except housing subsidies. The Secretary of State for the Environment is required to consult with local authority associations and to take account of:

1 Current levels of prices, costs and wage awards and any likely variation in these during the period of the grant. This allows the government to determine cash limits in order to ensure that local government adheres to government pay policies.
2 Any likely change in the demand for services which might affect the grant, eg, the declining birthrate, will affect the demand for education.

3 The need for developments and the extent to which it is reasonable to develop them. Thus the Secretary of State for Education and Science can claim to have included an extra 10,000 teachers in the RSG negotiations to develop in-service education. As we shall see, the equation is not as simple as that.

After negotiation the extent of central government aid is calculated as a percentage of the relevant expenditure and in recent years has been around 60 per cent. Specific grants, mainly to the police, are subtracted and the remainder is distributed under a complicated tripartite formula.

The three elements of this formula are 'domestic', 'resources' and 'needs'. The domestic element is distributed not to the spending authorities but to the rating authority (in a county that will be the district council) to cushion the householder against rising costs. This element is common to all authorities but the resources and needs elements can have a different effect in different authorities. The resources element is meant to help the poorer authorities without penalising the richer. The government provides sufficient resources to bring those authorities with a below average rate product up to the average. There are criticisms of the way this works in practice; for instance, rateable values tend to be poor indications of the real wealth of an authority.

The needs element, which makes up about 80 per cent of the total, is distributed on the basis of so-called objective factors such as pupil numbers and road mileage. It attempts to relate the income of an authority to the claims upon it. The largest part of the needs element is based upon population with the next most important being the 'education units'.

There is one factor in all of this which is crucial; despite arguments in RSG negotiations for extra teachers, in-service education and so on, the resulting grant is to the authority as a whole and education has to fight with other services for its share of the cake. It is, of course, unlikely that an individual authority would get completely out of line but it is impossible to tell how much education expenditure comes from the rates and how much comes from RSG. However, as education features highly in the needs element the RSG will tend to finance a larger part of education than over services and as a very rough guide it could be said that only about 25 per cent of education spending comes from the rates.

Controlling public expenditure

Great concern has been expressed recently about the percentage of gross national product devoted to public expenditure and the comment is frequently made that the country cannot spend more than it is prepared to earn. Public expenditure has risen from about 5 per cent of GNP in 1900 to a little under 50 per cent at the present time. It is understandable therefore that the government should wish to control such expenditure, particularly in inflationary times. Careful planning is essential in order to ensure that public spending as a whole can be financed, that services meet real social and demographic needs and that priorities between services are reviewed.

In 1958 the other 'Plowden Committee' on the 'Control of Public Expenditure' recommended that there should be regular surveys of expenditure as a whole, including that of local authorities, looking at a period several years in the future in relation to likely resources. Ten years later a white paper set out a new system of presenting estimates to Parliament and the Public Expenditure Survey Committee (PESC) was born.

This committee reviews expenditure on the basis of continuing current policies and then takes into account bids from service ministries for development, a similar process to that going on in the local authorities. This process is completed by mid-summer and it is then up to the cabinet to decide what policy changes the government desires and what level of expenditure the country can afford. Towards the end of the year the Public Expenditure White Paper will be published.

We have now reached a point where the local authority has guidance from the Public Expenditure Paper about the level of growth or reductions envisaged in its services, it knows in total the RSG being allowed and it has prepared total estimates based on continuation policies and developments. Before the full council meets to decide on the level of expenditure for the following year, the developments or cuts necessary and the rate demand, one other item must be fed into the financial equation – recoupment.

Recoupment

Recoupment is a process by which one authority pays another for the use of its services, usually the cost of providing education for children across a border. It would be difficult to gauge the total cost of every individual place, therefore agreed standard rates are suggested by an inter-authority payments committee. Other sums of money may be recovered by 'recharging' other departments for their services, notably social services and area health authorities.

There remain three areas where local authorities share expenditure by paying a set sum according to child population into a 'pool' and then drawing from it according to need. These pools are for initial and some in-service training of teachers, advanced further education and the 'no area pool' which covers students who have no 'home' authority, such as the children of travellers or whose parents live abroad.

Where does the money go?

It should now be clear that, although a refusal to grant a headteacher more money to improve his remedial provision might seem to be a naive and heartless attitude on the part of the LEA, the constraining factors on expenditure are both detailed and complicated. The individual primary head might only want £500 but, in total with all the other heads who require £500 across the country, this could represent a considerable drain on the nation's resources.

Furthermore the budgetary discretion of LEAs is limited. The total percentage spent on primary education nationally is about 29 per cent compared with 23 per cent for secondary education. Administration and inspection account for a further 4 per cent and FE, teacher training, and related expenditure (meals, transport, etc) account for all but 12 per cent of the remainder.

However, that 12 per cent comprises debt charges, or interest, on schools already built and is, therefore, an area over which the LEA has no discretion. We have seen that education is a major employer, therefore nationally agreed salaries have to be paid. Other parts of the service are provided by statute, eg, transport, school meals, mandatory awards, and in effect only something like 15 per cent of the education budget is truly discretionary.

It is in this area that cuts are usually made and LEAs can be as mean or as generous as they like. Unfortunately it is also from this area that many of the essential components that make a school or education service effective are financed. An LEA has discretion about where on the Burnham range it fixes the number of points available to a school, with obvious effects on staff recruitment and school organisation. It also has discretion over the amount of maintenance given to its properties and the strength of its advisory and support services. In particular it has discretion over the level of capitation allowances.

School income

The procedures outlined above will settle the overall level of resources in any one education authority and will determine the staffing allocation of a school and other centrally controlled expenditure. However, when it comes to cash in hand the head is usually faced with his capitation allowance, possibly supplemented by 'unofficial' school funds, with which to implement his curriculum policies. Traditionally, and in many cases remaining so today, the development of policy and its implementation financially has been solely in the hands of the headteacher. Too often scarce resources are not taken into consideration when making decisions about policy and yet it is surely impossible to separate a school's objectives from the money available to fulfil those objectives. At the very least, therefore, it is essential for heads to think of their capitation as a means to an end and not as a piggy bank which can be dipped into from time to time.

Capitation allowances are allocated to schools according to a scale determined by the LEA. It is a source of irritation to primary heads that an infant child is often worth only 50 per cent of a sixth former although when the specialist expenditure needs of secondary schools are considered the differential appears a little more reasonable. Nevertheless there are signs that the gap is beginning to narrow a little. The amounts allocated for day-to-day expenditure vary from LEA to LEA and as they may be intended for different specific functions it is difficult to compare one part of the country with another. Schools usually have discretion over spending on such things as textbooks, equipment and materials, consumable goods, servicing and hire of equipment, games visits and special expenses. Sometimes library books and furniture are included and sometimes specific grants are made for these items. In some areas cleaning materials and even postage are included within capitation allowances on the assumption that heads are more likely to control such expenditure if directly educational needs might benefit. Occasionally additional allowances are given to individual schools to cater for specific needs.

Most LEAs give heads detailed advice about their expenditure from capitation but it is worth bearing in mind that purchase through consortium or authorised suppliers can sometimes be at a discount and that VAT can often be reclaimed through the LEA. Schools are usually given regular, often monthly, computer tabulations of their expenditure as an aid to financial control.

Although capitation is the main source of income for a school, LEAs will probably retain some funds centrally for curriculum development. This may be disbursed through the advisory service, or schools may be able to make direct bids for planned expenditure.

In addition to the funds provided by the local authority, there are usually other funds created for the benefit of the school and its pupils known as 'unofficial school funds'. These will usually be raised by PTAs, school functions, sponsored walks and so on, although a few schools ask parents to make a termly or annual donation to the school fund. If carried too far the latter practice is difficult to support as education is a 'free service' apart from rates and taxes.

The responsibility for such funds rests with the head and governors as the recipients or custodians of the money. Usually the only requirement of the LEA is that a certificate of audit be submitted annually to the chief education officer covering all such funds, certifying that normal approved audit practices have been followed. In the case of voluntary schools there may be other monies available for the benefit of the school and its pupils which are held by the trustees of the fund. These are administered quite separately from the local authority and an audit certificate for these funds is not normally required by the authority.

Much of the unofficial school fund will be raised in one way or another from the parents but it often seems that the same parents dig deeply into their pockets time and time again and repeatedly man the stalls at the summer fête or the Christmas fayre. It is worth reflecting on how many times in a year parents are asked to contribute to the school for such things as Christmas parties, school photographs, summer camp or visits, touring theatres, collections for the blind, Miss Smith's leaving present and so on. The list seems endless and not only is the cost to the individual sometimes large but regular demands can be irritating and counter-productive. It may be better, therefore, to have one or two major fund-raising events each year, keeping other financial requests to a minimum.

Most schools receive relatively little income other than capitation, school fund and the very occasional donation. Official income usually occurs under the following headings:

1 Sales of work, materials, etc. Materials not brought to school or purchased by pupils for practical work are charged against capitation allowance so finished articles which pupils wish to take home can be charged for and the income set against expenditure.
2 School meals: monies collected for this purpose should be banked promptly.
3 Private telephone calls: if postage and telephone charges are set against capitation, private calls should be charged for to offset the school's expenditure.
4 Lettings: the letting regulations of some LEAs allow governors to levy additional charges in appropriate cases to provide additional income for school purposes.

School expenditure

In reviewing his expenditure the primary head will be grappling in miniature with the same problems faced by the LEA and the DES administrator: how can scarce resources be best allocated to forward the chosen policies of the school? As with central resources one cherished project, a staff library for instance, can only be afforded at the expense of something else, for example, new PE equipment. Priorities have to be decided and decisions made. How a head does this will depend on his style of leadership. The head carries great responsibility for establishing priorities between competing claims and some heads prefer to share this decision-making with their colleagues, or at least consult them before the final decision is taken.

However, in other schools a head will remain secretive about his resources, perhaps asking staff at some stage in the year what they would like and then deciding in an arbitrary fashion whether or not they can have it. In other schools staff will only be given resources if they actually take the initiative. Not only does such a management policy build up frustration and jealousies among staff but it also makes a nonsense of sensible planning and financial responsibility.

An alternative strategy employed by heads is to allocate a set amount to each teacher per term or year, possibly weighted to allow for class sizes or specialist responsibilities. This has the advantage of fairness and openness but if carried out too rigidly it can stifle experimentation and innovation and lead to a situation where no teacher can purchase major items for re-equipping his classroom. It also has the danger of allowing teachers to purchase conflicting schemes or projects and filling stockrooms with science kits which are only used for one year before the teacher concerned is promoted.

There is really no substitute for a regular review, with staff, of school policies and resource allocation. Before this is done funds should be set aside for consumable items, although there is also room for review with regard to this category. An 'emergency' fund should also be allocated to cover any unforeseen expenditure during the year. Sufficient money will also have to be set aside for any projects which are to be carried forward from previous years and which require continuing expenditure. These items can be seen as the school's continuation budget, allowing present policies to be carried forward for a further year.

What remains is the development budget and it is in this area in particular that staff discussion is essential. Much of this investment will have long-term implications and will have an effect on future policy decisions. Many of the projects considered for this money will be on a continuing basis needing injection of materials or equipment over a period of several years. A carefully planned and timetabled programme is desirable if the investment is to be fully effective. When these programmes are being considered the aims and objectives of the school must be central to the discussion. When resources are limited priorities have to be decided which are consistent with overall aims.

One of the basic management dilemmas is the amount of freedom that should be given to junior colleagues. We have seen in an earlier chapter how educational management differs from some other forms of management in the degree of professionalism involved in personal relationships. Too much freedom results in stock being purchased and rarely used; too little freedom leads to a dulling of initiative and a lack of personal involvement. What is necessary is participation in the setting of aims, and in resource decisions to reach those aims, while at the same time allowing for individual initiative and enthusiasm.

There is one final point for consideration about the question of allocating financial resources within primary schools, and that is in-service education. Teachers tend to 'spot' courses during the year which they would find useful and frequently return from them fired with new ideas and anxious to purchase the materials to put their ideas into practice. However, they find when back in school that no money is available and the ideas generated by the course never take hold. If in-service education is planned in a coherent way as part of overall staff development and policy implementation then the right courses would be attended and resources would be planned accordingly. Sometimes schools are allocated extra resources from the LEA when a member of staff returns from a course but unless attendance at the course has been considered as part of the school's policy the situation might arise that the school's aims are being unduly influenced from without. To be effective in-service training needs to be planned and the follow-up needs to be resourced.

Devolution of financial responsibility

So far we have been mainly concerned with how a head should deploy the capitation resources at his disposal. However, it is becoming more common for LEAs to give greater flexibility and discretion to headteachers to transfer expenditure from one budget heading to another. In this way heads have more control over the total resources available to their school. Such 'alternative use of resources' or 'virement' schemes should be discussed with and have the cooperation of the staff, especially where savings made through the deferment of appointments are 'vired' for materials or equipment. Used with care virement can allow a head to become a more effective manager provided that colleagues are aware of its reasons and understand the principles by which the decision was reached. Most authorities running virement schemes expect savings to be planned in one heading before they can be allocated to another. Fortuitous and retrospective savings are not usually entertained.

7 The Teaching Staff

Without doubt it is the teachers in a school who are the key to its success or failure. The best manager in a head's position is only as good as his staff will allow him to be, and despite the well-worn catch-phrase 'Johnny learned maths in spite of his teacher', even the brightest children need their work programmes developed, analysed and evaluated. To achieve the maximum results a head has two options:

1 To appoint new staff to suit his aims and objectives.
2 To develop existing staff to work towards the agreed policy.

The first choice seems the easier option but with falling school rolls and decreasing mobility on the part of teachers there will probably be fewer vacancies over the next few years, unless public expenditure is significantly increased to create more jobs. Even if you are fortunate enough to have vacancies to fill there is still a long road to travel before the successful appointment can be made.

Advertising

Whenever there is a vacancy in your school you should consider very carefully whether the new incumbent should be given the same responsibility as his predecessor. This will provide you with an opportunity to give flexibility to curriculum innovation and to the composition of the staff. Before the existing teacher leaves it is important to carry out with him a review of his basic teaching job and any extra responsibilities which he has undertaken. The aim of this review is to see which parts of the job can perhaps be discontinued, which parts are essential, and which parts can be dealt with more appropriately by another member of staff. The job should then be put into the context of the school's developing policy and from this some idea of the responsibilities of the new post can be discerned, together with the qualifications and experience that the ideal candidate should have.

Far too often a vacancy is filled without any real thought about the type of teacher required, the job specification, and how the job fits in to the school organisation. Not only should these points be clear to the head, but also to other senior staff and the governing body, especially the interviewing panel. The panel at the very least should be equipped with a specification for the job to be done and the sort of person who can do it. Without this the members have no means of objectively evaluating the candidates. Remember that a Scale 1 teacher aged twenty-five can cost an LEA £4,000 to employ which, multiplied over forty years, means a total investment of £160,000. This is a lot of money to throw away on a careless twenty-minute interview.

Once the job itself has been assessed the next stage is to attract a good field of suitable candidates. Although this might seem straightforward it can be quite difficult. The aim is to dissuade those without the necessary qualifications or experience from applying without putting off those who would do a good job.

Candidates are attracted through two separate but interlocking actions, the advertisement and the job description. Often the nature of the advertisement will be taken out of the headteacher's hands and the journals in which it is placed will be specified by the LEA, as will its format. Even if this is the case make sure you know what your LEA's policy is regarding advertisements. Which papers does it advertise in, does it circulate all LEA schools with current vacancies, does it run a mailing list and are you permitted to advertise locally?

If you are allowed to compose your own advertisement

remember that in just a few words you must both inform the candidates about the nature of the post and at the same time impress them that the job is for them. It is perhaps wise at this stage not to put off candidates with phrases such as 'special diploma essential' but to concentrate instead on a general impression of the vacancy.

It is in the job specification sent to candidates that fuller information can be given which will allow for a form of self-selection by the candidates. The basic policy is honesty: be accurate about the opportunities and problems of the job, the school and the area. The job specification should leave no doubt about the exact nature of the job, its responsibilities and where it fits into the school's overall philosophy, because the aim at this stage is to attract those who are genuinely interested in the vacancy. For the same reason it is helpful to give some guidance as to the sort of experience and additional qualifications which would be an advantage to the candidate.

Selecting the short-list

It is a daunting task to reduce fifty or more applications to a short-list of six. This is usually done in two stages: a long list of candidates for whom references are taken up and from this a final short-list to be interviewed.

During the job analysis stage you will no doubt have formed an impression of the ideal candidate for the job and your long list should reflect this. Occasionally heads will proudly boast about how they reduce the candidates list by discarding the bad writers, the poor spellers and so on but the task should really be done in a more systematic way. One way of achieving this is to use a simple points system for various factors which are seen as relevant to the vacancy. If nothing else this ensures that each application is carefully read and analysed. It is time-consuming, but then the appointment of staff is one of the most important tasks a headteacher undertakes.

It will be necessary to amend the points system for each job but typical factors might be:

Age

21–25	(2 points)
26–35	(3 points)
35–40	(2 points)
over 40	(1 point)

Qualifications

B.Ed.	(2 points)
Open University degree	(3 points)
Open University diploma	(2 points)
Special education diploma	(2 points)
One term secondment	(1 point)

Experience

More than five years in primary	(2 points)
Scale 2 experience	(3 points)
Special education experience	(2 points)
Urban experience	(2 points)
Large school experience	(2 points)

When the scores are added up the more suitable candidates should be apparent. However, always be careful not to ignore the border-line cases or those whose scores are reduced significantly by one factor such as age.

Having reviewed the applications and agreed a long list the next stage is to seek references on the chosen candidates. The most important references are, of course, from the head of the candidate's previous school or, where appropriate, a reference from the LEA. You should always be doubtful about a candidate who does not wish to include his existing employer as a referee. Although character references from the vicar, youth club leader, or bank manager can be used as supporting evidence, it is highly unlikely that a candidate would use one of these as a referee if they were expected to express a poor opinion of him.

Very occasionally a good reference will be written to get rid of a poor candidate, or a poor one written to keep a good teacher, but fortunately these cases are rare. The vast majority of references are honest and meant to be helpful, although the reader must be prepared to dig deeply into what might be meant between the lines of the reference, and what might have been omitted. A good reference will always be relevant to the job description (which should be sent to referees for their guidance) and caution should be exercised over a reference full of the good timekeeping and good health of a candidate but lacking anything about his ability actually to do the job. Ideally a reference should confirm what the candidate has already written in his application and should also provide additional relevant information. References should be written, but the telephone can be used to discuss a particular point or to ask for more information.

Many authorities no longer request testimonials. The difference between a testimonial and a reference should be clearly understood. A testimonial is an open letter setting out a candidate's strengths whereas the reference is a confidential appraisal of his ability to perform the job for which he has applied. While the testimonial might be helpful in drawing up the long list it cannot substitute for the reference at the short-list stage.

So the chosen few have been selected and have been invited for interview. The next stage begins.

The interview

The day of the interview can be stressful for both the applicant and the interviewing panel. Your main aim should be, therefore, to leave as little to chance as possible. Applicants should be given clear instructions about the reporting time and how to find the school plus, if necessary, information on where to stay overnight. A little thought here can pay a large dividend; if three candidates are coming from the Home Counties don't ask them to arrive ten minutes before the London train is due at the station.

It is important that candidates should be given the opportunity to see the school, ask questions of the staff, and get an idea of the school's structure and organisation. Invite them to report during the morning and arrange lunch for them at the school. This morning session can be valuable in a number of ways. Interviews should be a two-way process and it is reasonable that candidates should themselves be able to assess whether or not the job is for them. This can save time during the formal interview and may avoid the making of a disastrous appointment. On the other hand a lot can be seen of a person's personality and his rapport with children and staff as he is shown around. Allow the candidates time to talk to teachers and children as well as time to themselves. Research has shown that the best predictors of a person's performance are his potential colleagues so it can be useful at least to have an idea of which candidates 'click' with your staff.

The organisation of the day should be made clear to the applicants – the order of interview, who will be on the panel and so on. Remember that the members of the panel may be as tense as the candidates and possibly more unsure of themselves. Invite them to attend before the interview day for a briefing or, if that is not possible, leave a reasonable period of time before the interview itself to have a discussion with the panel.

The composition of the panel will depend on the regulations laid down by the LEA and the articles of government. If possible avoid an over-large panel and try to dissuade every member of the governing body turning up for a Scale 1 interview. Not only is this intimidating to a young teacher but much time can be wasted by asking irrelevant or duplicated questions.

Arrange to have available for the briefing a duplicated curriculum vitae of each candidate for all the panel members. Go through each one briefly so that the panel has an overall view of the people to be seen. Do not discuss any in detail at this stage, or read references, or suggest who the favourite might be. Try to keep the appraisal as objective as possible all the way through. Next, decide who will chair the panel and who will do the fetching and carrying. Finally, and most important, lay down the ground rules for questions. The aim of this is to give all members the chance to ask a key question, to make sure that all important issues are covered, to avoid people asking the same question in different ways, and to persuade the panel not to waste time asking such questions as, 'will you live in the village?' It is, of course, quite reasonable to allow panel members to come in with supplementaries but a basic framework should be agreed upon.

A small but important factor is the layout of the interviewing room. The candidate must be made the centre of attention without having the room look like an interrogation cell. If possible remove surplus furniture and avoid having panel members sitting behind bookshelves or desks. A simple semi-circle arrangement is better than a formal straight line. The light should be considered as it is quite unfair to expect a candidate to concentrate while blinking in strong sunlight, which is also silhouetting the people against the window.

When the candidate comes in the chairman should put her or him at ease; a couple of minutes can be spent breaking the ice through informal conversation, but it should be made clear that this is not part of the main interview. After this the major part of the time should be spent in listening to the candidate talking about her experience, how she views the job, and her opinion on other relevant matters. Some panel members like the sound of their own voices more than the candidates' so the chairman must be tactful but firm if this happens. Two things are important at the conclusion of the interview. Allow the candidate a few moments to ask questions of the panel which are relevant to the job. You should avoid getting into a long discussion about job prospects for the candidate's spouse, or the price of houses – these questions can be answered by your deputy. Second, ask the candidate if, after seeing the school, meeting the staff, being interviewed and given the opportunity of asking questions she still wants the job, if it is offered. This can save an embarrassing time later in the afternoon for all parties.

At the conclusion of each interview give the panel time to write down brief notes. It is much better that they do this rather than rely on memory. Full discussion and the reading out of references is best left to the end. When all the candidates have been seen the chairman should relate their strengths and weaknesses to the vacancy and all the members should be expected to comment. Often a consensus will quickly emerge but the paramount view must, of course, be given to the headteacher. One cardinal rule is, however, if in any doubt do not appoint. The time lost and the cost involved in re-advertising is small compared with that of making the wrong appointment.

Staff development

A school's manpower should not be left to their own devices whether they are newly appointed members of staff or teachers of many years' standing in a school. A head must accept the responsibility for staff appraisal, guidance and development even if in practice the operation of this is delegated to another senior member of staff. Such guidance and development is particularly essential in the case of probationary teachers although the assistance of LEA advisers is more likely to be available in that instance.

New teachers, whether new to the profession or not, must be guided through a period of induction into the school, the local authority and its resources. They should be encouraged to feel part of the organisation as quickly as possible and they should be shown that they have a particular contribution to make to the philosophy and objectives of the school. Probationers will also need additional pastoral help in the early terms although it is better if this is unobtrusive. Most probationers are better off staying away from any intensive in-service education during the first year; they have enough to do in relating their initial training to the demands of their first job.

Headteachers should undertake a continuous evaluation of an individual's training needs but a formal annual appraisal interview is very advantageous. This will allow the teacher to discuss, without prejudice, any problems he is having in pursuing the school's objectives, and his personal hopes for the future. The head will be able to assess, with his help, areas in need of improvement and areas of strength which may be of benefit to other members of staff. Suitable in-service education can be discussed for the coming year, together with ways in which the teacher can continue to make a positive contribution to the school as a whole, beyond his own classroom. The aim of the appraisal should be to build on existing strengths and to agree where extra help could be valuable.

In-service education can be of value to three different groups, although often the advantages are interwoven. An LEA can promote training to institutionalise new policies, such as secondary reorganisation, assessment or mathematics guidelines. A head can encourage teachers to attend courses which will be of direct benefit to the school, either in adopting common policies and philosophies among staff or in filling existing gaps. Third, individual teachers may wish to attend courses for promotional purposes.

The reasons why teachers attend courses should be clearly analysed and the benefits to school and individual assessed. Sometimes the disruption caused to routine is not worth the course because even if your LEA has a generous supply cover a regular change of teacher may not be in the children's interests. All these things are part of the managerial responsibility of a head.

It is a truism to say that those who go on courses do not need to, and those who never attend a course should. Regular and frank appraisal interviews will help to overcome this problem by setting the correct development objectives for each teacher.

If the aim of a course is to improve school or classroom performance, what happens at the conclusion of the course is even more important than its content. Heads should be aware of the content of the courses which staff are attending and should recognise any resource or organisational implications of follow-up. Ideally courses which are to benefit the school as a whole should be school-based or, in the case of small isolated schools, federally based. If this is not possible ample time should be allowed for staff discussions at the conclusion of the course and resources should be allocated to put ideas into practice. Above all, in-service education should not be carried on in isolation but should be firmly rooted in staff and school development.

As suggested earlier staff development is a continuing process and the provision of a small but carefully selected staff library can encourage new developments and introduce points for discussion. A feature should be made of any new books purchased and teachers should be encouraged to read and discuss them. A staff subscription to *Junior Education* or *Child Education* can also promote discussion of articles in the staffroom.

Visits to other schools should be encouraged, including those in other phases of education. This can be particularly helpful to teachers in isolated areas, offering them a comparison of practices and the chance to discuss their problems with colleagues.

Consultation

An earlier chapter emphasised that it was necessary for all teachers to pull in the same direction if common objectives were to be achieved. Consultation is part of the process of ensuring that everyone feels part of a team, and each individual knows what is expected of him. It can be achieved through informal contact and discussion and through the more formal forum of a staff meeting.

Informal consultation has its place but it is open to abuse unless its use is limited and the dangers clearly understood. A head will often wish to discuss a matter with his deputy but sometimes other teachers would be able to contribute meaningfully to the debate if given the opportunity. Even more dangerous, but an easy trap to fall into, is the consultative use of informal hierarchy where a teacher senior in age, or years of service, becomes the head's sounding board. This will inevitably lead to frustration and jealousy on the part of other members of staff.

In the end there is nothing that can replace a regular, formal staff meeting. Even in the smallest schools the setting of a regular time, with an agenda, can ensure more effective communication than relying on a chat over the mid-morning cuppa.

The content of staff meetings varies from the trivial, which sometimes takes up the bulk of the time, to the setting of long-term aims. One way of overcoming the *ad hoc* nature of so many staff meetings is to fix a regular fortnightly or monthly time, after school, or possibly during an evening at home, for the discussion of major items. The agenda should be prepared and circulated in advance, and everyone should have the opportunity to place an item on it. If necessary supporting papers can also be circulated.

Such a process would ensure that time is set aside for major items and that teachers are aware of their commitments. It avoids the rush to find a time when everyone is available at short notice. The trivial items can still be discussed at more informal lunch-time staff meetings.

The setting of such a regular commitment, especially if extended occasionally as a social event, can go a long way to encouraging a team feeling among teachers and thus keeping morale high. It is quite likely that, as the commitment is accepted, small groups will wish to explore more important themes in depth and the sense of one school pursuing a common goal will be strengthened.

Staff deployment

The number of senior posts in a school will be determined by its size and the local education authority's generosity on the points range. However, when the opportunity occurs to review the responsibilities of senior staff the head should start from the basis of what is in the best interests of the school. Whether or not additional responsibilities are given to teachers not receiving Scale 2 or above will depend upon the particular circumstances of the school, but the nature of all delegated responsibilities should be relevant to the school's aims and objectives, and the relative priorities should be within these objectives.

An NFER survey of Nottinghamshire primary teachers published in 1978 showed that the most common additional responsibility was for the organisation of the school library (72 per cent of respondent schools) followed by language consultants (67 per cent). Music responsibilities led mathematics by 61 per cent to 48 per cent; needlework at 37 per cent was well ahead of science at 21 per cent, and tuck shop organisation not far behind at 18 per cent. The 1978 Primary Survey of HMI showed a similar high percentage for music and low percentage for science.

Now it may well be that scale posts should be used to attract musicians and that the place of science in the curriculum can be safeguarded without delegating specific responsibilities to an individual teacher. What is important is that heads do not accept these assumptions without careful thought and discussions with colleagues.

The position of the deputy head is a difficult one. In a sense he sits in a no-man's-land but if he acts wisely he can be a major force in the staffroom. It is important that he, more than any other teacher, is given a clear job description and responsibilities, and these must extend beyond organising the duty rota. In the sudden prolonged absence of the head he would be expected to take charge of the school so he should be as fully involved in policy and problems as possible. Responsibility for a major area of the curriculum will involve him in day-to-day contact with all the staff; this becomes important if he is to be seen as more than the head's personal assistant.

Discipline

Many of the readers of this book, taking up their first headships, will have received their initial training during the mid- and late sixties. This was a period of rapid expansion in training colleges with the result that this generation of teachers has been given a reputation for low standards. This seems to be quite unfair, as any close look at the teaching profession will show that it is among the older generation that problems can be found, resulting from a failure to meet new challenges, or frustration at seeing the opportunities for promotion passing them by. Any profession has its black sheep and its less-than-average practitioners, but demands for greater accountability are highlighting the situation among teachers. The problem is compounded by the declining birthrate affecting the size of the primary teaching force for the next ten years at least, resulting in redeployment of staff and demands for higher teaching standards. It is almost certain, therefore, that primary heads will need to face up to issues of discipline, redeployment or premature retirement with their teachers and this section looks at this problem in some detail.

LEAs will have written into articles of government the procedure to be followed in the event of a teacher being in danger of discipline or suspension. Before such a stage is reached the head should have attempted a number of things to improve the teacher's performance. This is not only good management but also common sense in observing the rules of the Employment Protection Act and the recommendations of the Advisory, Conciliation and Arbitration Services (ACAS).

Your local authority should have a written disciplinary procedure available for consultation by all teachers and it is essential to follow this in practice. The ACAS code emphasises that employees should be told clearly the conduct expected of them and the consequences of breaking the rules.

Disciplinary procedures should not be viewed primarily as a means of imposing sanctions but more as a way of encouraging improvement in ensuring that acceptable standards of conduct and capability are maintained. Normally discipline can be effectively maintained by example, advice, job training and informal reprimand. If a difficult situation arises, and they usually arise gradually, a detached look should be taken at the problem; can the teacher be held entirely to blame or are there circumstances in the environment or organisation which aggravate the difficulty? After a frank discussion, either some in-service education, a change of class or responsibility, or an opportunity to try something new may suffice for an improvement to occur. Such discussions, including informal reprimands, do not usually constitute part of a formal disciplinary procedure. However, the teacher should be advised of the conduct or standard expected in the future and of the probable consequences of a further breach of discipline or act of omission.

If after a reasonable period of time the informal reprimand and other positive measures have not succeeded in obtaining an improvement, the formal procedure as laid down by the LEA should be followed. Asking for help from an adviser or education officer at an early moment is essential as they may be able to offer a solution which eludes the head. At all events their early involvement will make the process easier to bear for all concerned.

Occasionally a teacher may have a grievance against one of his colleagues or even against you as the headteacher. The Contract of Employment Act legislates that every employee must be given a note specifying the manner by which he can seek redress. A standard procedure is now common in most of the country, with some local variations, and all heads should be aware of it and be knowledgeable about its provisions.

Redeployment

We all hope that as pupil numbers in primary schools decline, pupil–teacher ratios can be improved and standards of education enhanced. However, even if LEAs act generously in this way some redeployment of teaching staff between schools is going to be a common feature of primary education for a number of years. By early 1979 there were signs of a 5 per cent rise in the birthrate, but this will not begin to affect schools until 1984. During the previous decade the decline was 25 per cent in some parts of the country which means that the overall reduction in primary pupil numbers is not likely to be balanced out before 1990 at the earliest.

Again all LEAs will have redeployment policies, discussed and agreed with teacher associations, and the method of deciding which teachers should be redeployed will be agreed locally. There are some common factors: the credibility of a redeployment policy will fail if schools only wish to take advantage of the situation to transfer their least able teacher.

The overall needs of the school should be looked at in determining who should be nominated and this must be matched against known or likely vacancies in the area. The experience and aptitude of the teacher are also very relevant here.

If you have a vacancy it is likely that you will be approached by the authority to accept a redeployed teacher. Quite naturally you will be reluctant to give up your freedom to appoint from a short-list and you will probably be supported by your governors in this. Bear in mind, however, the personal plight of a teacher redeployed in mid-career through no fault of her own, and be as sympathetic as possible within the overall needs and organisation of your school.

More often than not redeploying teachers is solved amicably and quickly through volunteers, promotions, retirements or 'natural wastage'. If not, and the problem remains intractable, the new premature retirement scheme for teachers may be the answer.

Premature retirement

Regulations have now been approved which allow teachers who retire before the age of sixty to receive, in certain circumstances, their pensions on retirement. Before this no allowances, other than invalidity benefits, were payable before sixty. To qualify for premature retirement compensation (PRC) the local authority must agree that the retirement is attributable to redundancy or else is 'in the interest of the efficiency of the service'.

Teachers accepting PRC must be at least fifty and must have completed five years' reckonable service. They are then paid immediately the pension and lump sum to which their superannuation contributions entitle them, and this may be augmented by the local authority to cover a notional addition of years of service up to a maximum of ten. Some authorities only pay a percentage of the maximum, which in any case must not:

1 be more than the teacher's pensionable service;
2 bring the total pensionable service to more than forty years;
3 have the effect of extending pensionable service contributions beyond the age of sixty-five, ie, a teacher receiving PRC at fifty-eight could only get a maximum of seven added years.

Industrial action

It is a pity to close a staffing chapter on a note of discord but all managers have to accept the responsibilities as well as the powers of leadership. The 1970s saw a rise in industrial action among public sector workers, including health and education. Teachers in a number of areas were on strike at various times in the decade but perhaps the worst disruption came early in 1979 as a result of National Union of Public Employees' (NUPE) action by caretakers, cleaners, lunchtime supervisors and canteen staff. Working to contract by teachers in May 1979 brought further difficulties.

As headteachers you will probably be members of a teachers' union or association and in the event of industrial action by teaching or non-teaching staff your own union will usually offer guidance. At the same time your LEA may give you guidance or instructions which might conflict with union advice.

Your own personal views should be relegated in favour of the long-term needs of the school. Two things should be borne in mind and the action taken should depend on a consideration of them. Most important – what action is in the best interest of the children? The safety of each pupil must be secured and advance notice of any exclusions must be given to parents. Heads should assume responsibility for any children who arrive at school through a misunderstanding of the situation.

The second consideration is the long-term effect of the action on the school, and the need here is to ensure as far as possible that normal routines are re-established in an atmosphere of goodwill. Actions which will aggravate the situation should, therefore, be avoided, unless the safety of children is at risk or the loss of their education is becoming intolerable. With proper consultation at all levels it is surprising what agreements can be reached even during a period of industrial action. Heads should not undertake anything which can be construed as black-legging as this is certain to cause long-term bitterness. If possible, discussions held before the action takes place should determine what is or is not permissible. One should note here, however, that most LEAs regard it as the headteacher's responsibility to open the school, even though this may be delegated to caretakers for practical purposes.

It is the teaching staff who are in the front line of education and it is their work which is crucial to the whole process. Careful selection of staff, successful deployment to make the most of their various abilities, good consultation with them, together with an overall caring attitude towards their work are key tasks for the manager. If he is successful in this his school is off to a good start.

Remember also, staff will be judging the head – by his compassion, his sense of humour, his attitude to the children and by his sense of purpose.

8 Non-Teaching Staff

Schools exist for children to learn and this demands a close relationship between pupil and teacher. However, some critics of the education service point to the fact that only 50 per cent of the employees in the service are teachers, accusing schools and education departments of bureaucratic mismanagement. In fact less than 5 per cent of the salary bill is spent on central administration by LEAs, including advisory services; the rest goes on essential support to teachers in keeping classrooms clean and in meeting legislation in respect of school meals. In any primary school, therefore, it is likely that there will be as many non-teaching staff as teachers. Headteachers come from the ranks of assistants and it is natural for you to be more concerned with the actions of teachers than with the actions of other members of staff, but if a school is to run smoothly it is important for you to accept your responsibility as a manager, regardless of profession.

The caretaker and cleaning staff

'The power behind the throne' is a phrase sometimes used about school keepers, or caretakers, and it is true that some caretakers seem to exert more influence on the running of a school than the head. As in all walks of life there is a range of interest and ability among caretakers. Some can be particularly cantankerous, making life a misery for cleaning and teaching staff. If this is the case a headteacher must be prepared to make a stand for good management. But it is more often the case that a caretaker will not only do his allotted tasks in an efficient and friendly manner, but will also do a variety of extra jobs for the school at no extra charge. Such a man is worth his weight in gold.

The relationship between head and caretaker must be based upon mutual trust and as full an understanding as possible of each other's function in the school, including their respective tasks, frustrations and expertise. Heads should avoid a 'know-it-all' attitude; an approach recognising the particular knowledge of the caretaker will always be more effective. The recognition of the key role of the caretaker is important; in the day-to-day running of the school he is perhaps second in authority only to the headteacher. A possible source of conflict may arise in this connection because of different perceptions of authority with regard to role importance. It is not unknown for Scale 1 probationers to give orders to caretakers of many years' experience, and children will not be slow to play one member of staff off against another. Heads must be on the watch for any developments of this sort and they should be tactfully nipped in the bud.

The caretaker's main tasks are probably carried out when the academic staff are not on the premises, before 8.30 am and after 5 pm. At these times he becomes the representative of the school and the LEA, in effect the acting headteacher. Visitors are as likely to come to school at these times as any other, telephones will ring, crises will occur. Caretakers should therefore be aware of the importance of this role and the occasional discussion on meeting school visitors and dealing with telephone calls would not come amiss.

Under the caretaker, or cleaner in charge, there may well be other assistant staff. He is responsible for their deployment and has an important managerial function to perform in this connection. If he is wise he will want to be able to give his staff a 'pat on the back' and in the same way he also likes to know that his own efforts are appreciated. A regular 'thank you' or 'well done' goes a long way to encourage him to do that little bit extra the next time the school hall is used for a pet show.

It is possible that more time than should be will be spent by the caretaker on vandalism and damage. He will have a good deal of daily contact with the children and it is natural that he might see their presence in the school as being the only thing preventing it from always being clean and tidy. A broken window or blocked toilet can sometimes be the last straw. A good head will recognise this and will attempt a positive approach in using the caretaker to get through to pupils the problems, costs and inconvenience of vandalism.

Teachers, too, can unwittingly cause extra work for caretakers. Is it really sensible to leave pieces of clay all over the floor at the end of the last lesson on a Friday? Can little Johnny really be trusted not to empty the waste bin all over the junior playground? This is not to say that caretakers should determine curriculum or discipline, but merely that they should be one of the factors considered in reaching an operational decision.

To overcome these minor difficulties, which sometimes reach major proportions, personal contact is vital. An hour or so put aside each week for a cup of tea and a chat with the caretaker is well worth it. This might seem a large investment of time, but can be seen in proportion when set against the total number of hours available. It is much better than hoping for 'a word' at an odd moment. It is surprising how many things need to be discussed: how much cash is available for cleaning materials; how the cleaners are performing; what areas of the school or members of staff are creating cleaning problems; what planned school activities could intrude on the cleaning of the school; what repairs and minor building alterations are necessary; how can the central heating system be made more effective, and last but by no means least, how is his wife's lumbago?

Such an approach will foster a communal spirit, and it should be the aim of every head to have his staff working as one for the good of the school. The main function of the school in educating children will be achieved much more pleasantly if the surroundings are clean, tidy and well cared for, and if an 'us and them' approach between manual and non-manual staff is avoided.

The activities of the caretaker and cleaners should be outlined to the pupils to give them some idea of what is involved in maintaining a clean, warm school for their use and comfort. Not only will this make them more appreciative of the caretaker's work and hence more responsible in their use of the premises but it will also give the older ones some idea of the world of work. The caretaker's job and responsibilities can also be used as a teaching point.

Many LEAs already appoint teaching staff to their governing bodies and just a few include such non-teaching staff as caretakers. In any case the caretaker should be invited to the occasional governors' or PTA meeting, to see and be seen, to ask and answer questions and to state his views should any problem or query arise. He will be seen as, and will feel, a full member of the school staff.

The caretaker and his staff are a vital part of the school's day-to-day life. Should they fail in their duties, at best life in the school will be uncomfortable, at worst the school could be a health hazard. The head who accepts this and goes out of his way to encourage the spirit of belonging in *all* his staff will have a happy and clean school. A 'good evening' costs nothing but it does mean a lot.

School meals staff

As long as schools operate a full day, a catering service of some description will continue to be necessary. Some parts of the country have experimented with one-session days on the continental pattern but it is unlikely that such a practice will become common in view of this country's employment pattern for working mothers. Suggestions are also made, especially at times of economic difficulty, that the meals service should be transferred to social services departments. If this happened it is unlikely that the education budget would see any financial benefit, as the demand for the service would still need to be met. Neither would the management structure be made easier; school kitchens are expensive plant and in my view it is essential for a head to have overall responsibility for all the workers in his school, and all parts of the school, even if the canteen is linked to a county catering officer.

Many of the points made about caretakers and cleaning staff are also appropriate to the 'canteen and dinner ladies'. The staff employed to provide the meals service have a vital job to do and they are just as important as other staff. Because they provide a service they need motivation and if a head is to get the best out of these members of staff he must give them some daily attention, whatever his personal feelings.

This attention can be in various forms. A daily look into the kitchen to say 'good morning' is always appreciated, while sitting down for morning coffee with the meals staff once a week shows a real interest in their work. It is also important to help the children understand the work of meals staff by taking time to show and explain to them what the staff have to do to ensure that the meals are ready in time. Again, many teaching points can arise from this involvement; indeed a project on 'The working of the school' can be of more benefit than other themes more remote in time or place. Great use can be made of the kitchen when discussing food and foodstuffs with pupils. The opportunity should be grasped to illustrate what is 'good' and what is 'bad', why certain foods are offered and others not, etc. Why not take *organised* groups into the kitchen?

Contact made in ways such as these will encourage two-way communication between teachers and pupils on the one hand and non-teaching staff on the other. High morale and motivation for all must be the direct benefit of this.

Once a year, perhaps, the cook, like the caretaker, could be invited to a PTA or governors' meeting so that parents or governors can put their questions and worries directly to her. So often complaints about school meals are secondhand and coloured by a person's own school experience of twenty-five years ago. The opportunity to discuss difficulties at first-hand can do much to relieve problems.

Ancillary help

The concept of ancillary assistance is not new in an educational context although, mainly because of financial constraints, their use is perhaps not as widespread as it could be. These helpers have a variety of titles – auxiliary, teachers' aide, etc – but whatever the name the idea refers to persons who can aid professional teachers in their daily encounters with children in the classroom. The impetus for this move has come from teachers wanting relief from the more time-consuming and repetitive tasks reinforced by objective studies of how teachers spend their time. There are still a few heads and teachers who see the aides as a threat to the teacher's position in the classroom and there are others who feel unease at sharing a class with another adult. Those who feel threatened should reflect on their training and experience: they are the professional educators, the directors of programmes, the evaluators of work. Seen in this context aides can be a source of help by relieving teachers of routine non-teaching tasks and so increasing their direct contact with children. Unease at sharing a room with another adult is understandable, although it can stem from a sense of insecurity. Given time and good personal relationships on both sides it can usually be overcome.

It is clearly important that ancillaries do not cross the line between non-teaching and teaching work. They should not be used as substitute teachers, or on duties involving the organisation and management of classrooms, the planning of learning strategies, the assessment of pupils' needs or the evaluation of their progress. However, they can be of immense use in helping pupils with problems in using materials, especially giving encouragement during activity lessons. The preparation of work cards, paint and so on can also save the teacher a great deal of time.

One thorny problem is that of reading. Generally it seems quite appropriate for ancillaries to hear adequate readers when there is unlikely to be a fundamental learning problem. It is a different matter with a remedial group who will need specific help, attack skills and learning strategies.

The key to success in using ancillaries is the attitude of the head. Where the role is defined and made clear to all, including pupils, there is an even greater chance of real effectiveness. Teachers will have their own views about the amount of ancillary time that should be allocated to them and they should be consulted about their needs. Larger blocks of time do, however, seem to be more effective than shorter ones. It can be helpful to leave a couple of hours each week free from class responsibilities for the helper to be used on specific and irregular tasks.

The ancillary helper, like all non-teaching staff, should be regarded as a full member of the school staff. Use of the teachers' room (if the school has one!) can cause difficulties and teachers sometimes worry that their conversation and discussion will be inhibited by non-teachers being present. In the end the solution will depend on the size of the staff and the staffroom and the relationships which have been built up. However, a shared common room helps to create a better understanding and allows teachers to discuss their needs with the helpers.

All non-teaching staff – cleaning, cooking, ancillary, secretarial (of which more is said later) – need in-service training if they are to perform their duties to the best of their abilities. Often the opportunities for this training are rare. Heads should encourage their LEAs to mount relevant courses and facilitate the attendance at these courses by their manual staff. If no LEA course is available the occasional school-based course can do much to increase commitment to the job and is well worth a headteacher's time. He will often find that local authority staff are willing to help, especially superintendents of caretakers, catering officers, and nursery/infant advisers.

The emphasis in this chapter has been that to manage a school a head must be interested in the whole exercise and not just the educational side. This may be the end and the reason for the school's existence: however, the rest is part of the means of achieving that end.

9 Children with Special Needs

In May 1978 the first major government committee to consider the needs of the handicapped child produced its report. The recommendations made under the chairmanship of Mrs Mary Warnock will certainly shape special education for the rest of this century and will also have a significant impact on the organisation of ordinary schools. One of the more emotive parts of the special education debate has been the question of integrating handicapped children into the mainstream. This argument was legislated for in the 1976 Education Act which, in Section 10, states that all children should be educated in ordinary schools where it is in their best interests provided that this does not act to the detriment of the non-handicapped pupils and does not take an unreasonable amount of public expenditure.

The Warnock Report accepted the principle of 'Section 10' but was more concerned with the practical difficulties of integration. The consultations undertaken since the publication of the report seem to show that most authorities are pressing on with programmes for more integration but that the need for special schools will remain for the foreseeable future and their status enhanced by their development as resource centres. It is not only the individual child who needs to be integrated into the normal system but special education as a whole, and this is one of the main features of the report. Furthermore Warnock identified a large percentage of children as in need of special support, and most of these children are integrated already into ordinary schools. Which children are therefore in need of this special help, how can they be identified, and how are their needs to be met?

Who needs special help?

Children in need of special help, and formally ascertained under procedures laid down by the DES, are still categorised within the Schools Regulations made following the 1944 Education Act. These categories are:

Educationally subnormal (mild and severe);
Maladjusted;
Physically handicapped;
Delicate;
Partially hearing;
Deaf;
Partially sighted;
Blind;
Epileptic;
Speech defects.

After ascertainment by medical and psychological officers, a child is found a place in a school with the appropriate label. It has become quite apparent that such a system is restrictive in the opportunities it offers to the handicapped child and the emphasis, strongly backed by Warnock, is now to determine the environmental and curriculum needs of a child and to educate him in the most suitable way. Needs therefore become more important than the basic handicapping condition.

This is less than half the story, however, as the categories outlined above, and which Warnock is anxious to modify, cover less than 3 per cent of the school population. That 3 per cent has needs which require special teaching, a special curriculum, a special medical or social environment, or a particular form of treatment. This teaching may be provided in a special school or in an ordinary school but it is likely to be long-term with implications well beyond normal school leaving age.

It is proposed that the rather obscene label 'educationally subnormal' should be replaced by 'children with special learning difficulties', and these difficulties should be seen as severe (mentally handicapped children), moderate (children presently in the ESN(M) area) and mild (children in need of remedial help). The size and needs of the latter group are larger than was once appreciated and although the demand may be for relatively short-term help, limited to fairly specific objectives, nevertheless it has to be met. Among the school population as a whole one child in five might need some form of special educational treatment at some time during his school life, or compensation to make up for an inadequate educational environment outside school. Thus, the real demand for special education is much higher than the formal ascertainment of 3 per cent would suggest.

Identification and referral

The sooner a child's special needs are identified the better the chances of making adequate educational provision for them. A severely mentally handicapped child, and children with physical or sensory handicaps, will be recognised by parents or doctors well before school age. For some of these children a decision will be made to start schooling in the mainstream, possibly with extra support from ancillary helpers. The child's progress will then have to be carefully monitored to ensure that his needs really are being met in the ordinary school.

Children with less severe handicaps, and those with learning difficulties, may not be identified until the infant stage, or possibly even later. It is sound practice to use some form of screening device, such as a developmental checklist, which will assist teachers in deciding whether or not a child has a particular difficulty. A good checklist will include the observation of physical factors (eyesight, hearing, speech, coordination), perceptual difficulties (visual and auditory discrimination), linguistic problems (understanding stories and instructions), social/emotional demands (confidence, peer group difficulties) and direct responses to learning situations (interest, distraction, perseverance). The checklist should not only assist teachers in the identification of children with special needs but should also be diagnostic in pointing out how these needs can be met, and who should be approached for help.

It cannot be emphasised too often that a child's particular needs must be monitored throughout his school career. After careful assessment it may be decided that his education can be provided quite adequately in an ordinary class, but this must be a positive decision. It is quite wrong to let a child struggle in the mainstream when the school is not really able to meet his needs. With falling pupil numbers in primary schools it is true that their ability to cope with special problems will be improved; nevertheless this must be set against alternative forms of provision.

The use of a sophisticated developmental checklist, together with other school-based screening procedures, should lead to the identification of most difficulties. Some authorities are also taking up the recommendations of both Bullock and Warnock in starting the screening of whole age-groups of children, first at about seven, again towards the end of the junior stage, and sometimes at the options stage in the secondary school. Not only does this scheme provide another fail-safe device but it also enables a linear profile to be kept on each child, and allows for the comparison of reading quotients to be made across school boundaries. This can be particularly helpful at the transfer stage.

If a teacher is concerned about a child's progress, and this is confirmed by screening, the first step is to discuss with the headteacher whether the school can cope. If there is any doubt about this an advisory teacher or educational psychologist should be contacted for further advice. This is especially true for children with social or emotional problems which aggravate their learning difficulties. If it is thought that special education (SE) should be considered then the appropriate procedures, usually involving the completion of SE forms, should be set in motion. If continued placement in the ordinary school is thought best the psychologist and adviser should recommend learning programmes and strategies that can be used.

Two small points may have a significant part to play in success. If parents can be involved at an early stage, listened to, and shown how they can help, the chances of educational improvement are greatly enhanced. On the other hand the structure of the school, the curriculum, the attitude of staff to the child, should all be reviewed. This is not to say that a perfectly good organisation should be turned upside down to allow one child to settle. However, quite often a minor change on the part of the school can make a considerable difference to the child with special problems.

Support services

Advisory and support services are there to be used, despite lengthy waiting lists. Educational psychologists, social workers, medical officers, advisory teachers, all have a part to play in diagnosing difficulties and offering solutions. But they can only analyse a difficulty in proportion to the information they have. Before asking a psychologist or other adviser to see a child be sure to have discussed his problems internally. Prepare a brief report including in it all relevant test scores, the ways in which the problem has manifested itself and the strategies which have so far been applied. This will give the psychologist a sound base from which to approach the difficulty. You are then more likely to get back detailed suggestions for further help than a mere quotation of test scores and repetition of a problem you already know.

Special education provision

The Warnock Report advocates a continuum of special education provision from total integration in an ordinary school classroom to residential special school. Although many of the children in a school for the mentally handicapped, and to a lesser extent the physically handicapped, will never have attended an ordinary primary school, the wise headteacher will recognise that he is but a part of the education system. He will try to be aware of local special schools, arrange visits or even staff exchanges and encourage links between children. Physically handicapped children could, for example, be invited to share a touring theatre company's production with primary children. This will help the non-handicapped children to accept the problem of handicap in society. Such a venture must always be done very carefully and selectively, as a sudden influx of severely handicapped children can be very disturbing emotionally to the primary child.

The less severely handicapped child may be placed in a specialist class attached to an ordinary school. Such a class will be staffed by a specialist teacher of the handicapped (eg, the hearing impaired) and will be equipped with suitable aids and equipment (loops, speech trainers, phonic ears). Depending on their handicap, the children will spend part of the day in the special class and part in the ordinary school. Such classes are now widely available for the hearing impaired, but are much fewer in number for the visually and physically handicapped. A handful of LEAs are experimenting with special classes for mentally handicapped children.

A more radical type of provision is total integration with extra support if necessary. This is most common with physically handicapped children where specialist equipment is provided, building alterations are made, and welfare assistants are appointed to look after the physical needs of the children.

It should never be taken for granted that just because a

handicapped child is educated in a special class attached to an ordinary school, or even directly in the ordinary school, he is totally integrated. By being given different work to do, or being especially protected from normal rough and tumble, his particular difficulty can be highlighted. Heads must be quite clear that any handicapped child in their school is fully benefiting from the experience. Integration in the sense of location and placement is only part of the answer; integration must also be considered from the social and educational point of view. Furthermore the integration of pupils is not enough: the integration of specialist and main school staff must be complete, and the integration of the parents of the handicapped, who may come from a much wider catchment area than the main school parents, is also essential.

Dyslexia

One of the most emotive types of handicap which the primary head may have to deal with is 'dyslexia'. Not only is the handicap itself open to some question but its particular links with the so-called 'middle class parent' tend to hide the real problem. Some headteachers, psychologists and educational administrators believe that it is only a question of such parents trying to make their child's reading problem sound respectable. One correspondent to a national paper went so far as to suggest that the only way to get dyslexia accepted by the authorities was to 'visit the Child Guidance Clinic, hair in rollers and dog-end in mouth, reeking of stout and saying as loudly and coarsely as possible that Wayne (a less dyslexic name than Rupert) can't read because he's thick and you haven't got time to keep bringing him to the clinic because you are missing bingo'.

Be that as it may it is clear that there are some children, of apparently good intelligence, who suffer from a specific reading problem. The literal meaning of the word dyslexia is 'difficulty with reading' but a neurologist would define it as a 'disorder which, despite conventional classroom experience, prevents children from attaining skills in reading, writing and spelling', thus implying an underlying neurological cause.

The argument between medical and non-medical opinion about the existence of an identifiable dyslexic condition has been continuing since 1890 and there seems little sign of it abating. The basic error made by many people is to assume that dyslexia is not simply a word which describes a problem but rather a diagnosis indicating the underlying cause of the problem. The busy class teacher, or primary headteacher, just does not have the time to enter into such a philosophical discussion. When a child shows classic 'dyslexic symptoms' (b–d confusions; letters in the wrong order; leaving letters out of a word; apparently 'careless' reading errors; difficulty in coping with arithmetical tables, etc) the teacher should be more concerned with helping than labelling.

Reading failure of itself cannot be a disease as reading is a process of modifying behaviour and learning a skill. Failure to learn that skill is not an organic disability. The basic causes of reading failure are so complex that one single term for it is a gross oversimplification, ignoring many other contributory factors such as personality, emotions and motivation.

A child with apparent 'dyslexia' should be given the same support as any other child with a learning difficulty. If it helps the parents to call their son 'dyslexic' then so be it, but the job of the school is to identify the problem, propose and implement suitable remedial action, and if necessary refer the child for specialist help. Parents of 'dyslexic' children often rush to the media to claim that their local authority does not recognise dyslexia. What they really mean is that their LEA will not pay for their child to attend an independent school. Many authorities have well-structured channels for dealing with this difficulty and heads are advised to acquaint themselves with local practice.

The gifted child

Special help seems sometimes to be more than adequate for the less able pupil but a common feeling is that the brightest child can take care of himself. Increasing concern has been shown recently at the curriculum offered to gifted children in comprehensive schools and the 1978 HMI Primary School Survey suggested that bright children were not stretched enough. There is now an increasing awareness that these children have special educational needs and they are becoming a greater focus of concern among teachers.

There is probably a significant number of gifted children who remain unrecognised in the primary school. This is likely to be more common among schools in deprived areas as environmental deprivation has been shown to have its greatest effects on the academic attainment of the brightest children, not the average or dull ones.

There is no common consensus about the definition of a gifted child. A generally agreed baseline is an IQ of 145 in a reliable test, but the abilities of the specifically gifted, especially the creative, must not be ignored. Furthermore, a child could well be gifted without the fact being made evident either generally or specifically. Teachers should therefore be alert to signs of specific ability and be prepared to investigate further. They should also be willing to give a reliable test to any child who has shown himself generally gifted during whole age-group monitoring. This is why a screening exercise should have a high cut-off point to suggest the most able as well as a low one to identify the least able.

A gifted child may have problems with personal rela-tionships as well. Close cooperation is required between parent and school and the head should strive to establish an understanding and sympathetic relationship. Within the school attempts should be made to allow the child to maintain normal contact in everyday activities with children of his own age range. The gifted child should not be set apart, but should be given the opportunity to work alone on occasions, and to join with children of comparable ability on special courses if these are available. Above all he should be subject to a high level of expectation and he and his parents should have regular counselling available through school and from other specialists. To meet these particular needs the school must be willing to tap all the available resources which will allow the child to carry out a sophisticated programme while the internal organisation must be sufficiently flexible to allow him the opportunity of sufficient enrichment within everyday school life.

A school which develops an ethos in which qualities of leadership, creative thinking and artistic ability are nurtured will set itself high standards and will encourage the gifted child. A school which develops a philosophy of caring for all whatever their difficulties or handicaps will set itself compassionate standards and will encourage the less able or disabled child. There is no reason why these two should not go together in embracing the needs of all children within a general policy of considering them as individuals. In this way every child will be a special case, and those with special needs will be adequately provided for.

10 Beyond the School

Despite moves towards more open forms of democracy and attempts by many schools to become more involved in community life there still remains an us-and-them attitude between lay people and those involved professionally in education. Such a feeling even exists between some secondary schools and their feeder primaries. The Taylor Committee proposed basing governing bodies more firmly in the community but how far this exercise will go remains to be seen; far more is needed than a statutory parent and industrialist on the board of governors.

The only real and lasting way of overcoming this attitude is by involving the school in the life of the community, and the community in school activities. What happens beyond the school gates is of vital importance to the health and success of a school. External relationships should be encouraged, nurtured and monitored. Those who fear undue interference on the grounds that a little learning is a dangerous thing should recognise that the alternative is frustration and ignorance which can prove to be a much more explosive mixture. External relations must be carefully controlled to avoid cliques, favouritism and prejudice but if managed with sensitivity they can help to ensure a smoothly running school. Like all other management activities external relations must be planned, organised, controlled and evaluated.

The world beyond the school gates can be conveniently divided into three areas (relationships with LEA, teachers' unions, etc, have already been discussed). These are parents; the educational community; and the non-educational community.

106

Working with parents

Reports ranging from Hadow[1] in 1931 to Warnock[2] in 1978 have emphasised that deprived homes can seriously prejudice a child's knowledge of language and communication skills, and thus the whole foundation of education, while on the other hand supportive homes help children to enter school with the foundations well laid. Researchers such as Douglas[3] have backed these reports, suggesting that children can acquire at home almost as much information about the world as they can at school. Thus every opportunity should be taken to make clear to parents the very great importance of supportive attitudes in the first five and subsequent years of a child's life.

The first five years are of crucial importance, and the good primary school can play a central role in guiding parents through these difficult years. Good contact with local playgroups can be a great advantage and some schools have arranged meetings of parents with the cooperation of maternity and health clinics. If parents can be encouraged to have a supportive attitude to school when their child is a 'pre-five' it is likely that they will work for the school's good when their child attends full-time. Schools can still be forbidding places for young parents so it helps if early meetings with head and staff can be on neutral premises, such as at a playgroup or clinic.

Great care is now taken over the medical needs of babies but much less over their educational needs. 'Mother and Toddler' groups have proved to be successful in encouraging mothers to talk and play with their children and if a primary school can encourage and assist in this sort of activity it will reap benefits

---

[1] *Primary School Report by the Consultative Committee of the Board of Education*: its brief was "To inquire into and report on courses of study suitable for children (other than infants) up to 11 in elementary schools, with special reference to needs of children in rural areas."

[2] *Special Educational Needs: report of the Committee of Enquiry into the Education of Handicapped Children and Young People.*

[3] *Home and the School* by James William Bruce Douglas (MacGibbon & Kee, 1964).

107

from both parents and children at the time of school admission.

Even when a child is attending school full-time he only spends about 27 per cent of his waking hours there. Unless there is cooperation and support from home the work of the school can be quite useless. But it is all too easy for a head to complain that he has no cooperation, or that 'the parents you want never come'. There will be many frustrating times when no meaningful dialogue can be opened, but in general good cooperation will come only from hard work.

The obvious way adopted by many schools is to set up a parent–teacher association and provided the PTA does not attempt to dominate the situation but is based on a harmonious relationship between the head, staff and governors, such organisations can be a source of strength and support to the school.

A parent–teacher association should not infringe on the professional rights of the head and his colleagues in the matter of the curriculum, syllabus, teaching methods, etc. On the other hand a parent–teacher association which is only involved in social activities may not justify the devotion by teachers of their energies and spare time to it. More fruitful is the middle way in which useful information about the school's aims and how it fits into the educational pattern of the area is disseminated, as well as information about what the school is trying to achieve. This should by no means be a one-way process but truly professional teachers can often gain insights into their job by listening to parents; listening is perhaps not ingrained in all of us.

In any case the aims of the association should be carefully set out so that everybody knows what can be done, and what cannot. If a formal association is to be set up some form of constitution will be necessary, if only to ensure the orderly conduct of meetings and the democratic election of officers. The National Federation of Parent–Teacher Associations can offer advice about this. It is best to avoid too formalised a structure otherwise bureaucracy will take over and the association will die a lengthy but definite death. Some associations spend endless time arguing about their name; should it include or exclude parents and teachers. It really is not worthwhile wasting time on this; call it the 'School Association' or 'Friends of the School' – presumably all teachers and parents will want to be friends of, or associated with, the school!

PTAs can be very valuable, but they are not necessarily the best means of fostering close relations between home and school. They can be valuable where good leadership is given by the head, but they may do harm if in the hands of a small group. There is also some evidence to suggest that certain parents are not good attenders at PTA meetings, so that may not be the best method of involving all concerned.

Above all parents need information – information about the school but particularly about their child's place in it. Comments on communicating with parents are made elsewhere in this book but a headteacher should never take significant action regarding a child or class without informing the parents and giving them the reasons. This is especially so when a child's class is changed, or where a new organisation is adopted, eg, vertical grouping. Parents' conception of school is based on their primary school days perhaps twenty years earlier and they may well not appreciate the organisation or curriculum of the 1980s.

Whatever device is adopted to suit local circumstances – a PTA, a parent association, friends of the school – or simply very active involvement with school affairs, the essentials are: to get parents into the school; for parents to meet teachers and see what the children are doing and why; to ensure that parents are well informed about the school in general and their own children in particular.

The following is a not exclusive list of the more obvious ways of stimulating parental involvement, with or without a PTA.

GENERAL INFORMATION
The national survey undertaken by the Plowden Committee showed that more than 30 per cent of parents did not see the headteacher before their children started school. The more information available to parents about the general organisation and running of the school the better (see A–Z section 'Admissions' p. 141 and 'Information for Parents' p. 146), but this is much more valuable if head and staff can take the time to meet new parents and allow children to visit the school before admission.

EDUCATIONAL MEETINGS
These meetings notoriously encourage only those parents with a special interest in their children's work, but they should not be ignored purely on this basis. It is precisely these parents with a little knowledge of education who can be most critical of the school's performance. Every way of giving them more information about the aims and methods of the school should therefore be used. Sessions can be held not only on curriculum matters but also on how parents can help their own children with reading and number, and what other activities can be encouraged at home. From time to time educational clinics could be held with teachers and others answering educational questions on an individual basis.

SCHOOL REPORTS
The value of reports is often underestimated as they can be the only way in which a parent is given some indication of how a child is progressing. Reports should be informative and should contain much more than just grades for performance. Comments on progress and development and suggestions about the ways in which parents can help to overcome their child's difficulties can involve them in the academic side of school. Some teachers present reports much more as a letter to parents rather than a forbidding pro forma, and add space at the bottom for parents to write their own comments. All this

takes time of course and therefore the report writing needs to be limited; there is no reason why this should be at the end of each term, or even at the end of the year. A report written, for instance, at the spring half-term can be used as a teaching tool in encouraging a dialogue between parent and teacher, rather than being just a certificate of course completion.

OPEN EVENINGS

Reports will be much more meaningful if allied to a reasonable system of 'open evenings'. These again are time-consuming but can be a very positive help to the teacher. Appointment systems seem to work best, provided times are kept to and queues of parents are avoided. It is also wise to avoid leaving children's books on display all over the room; parents are naturally inquisitive and will want to compare their child's work with other class members. However, an opportunity should be given to see the work of the school displayed, and possibly some activities actually in progress. It is impossible to find a time suitable for everyone so flexibility must be the key note. Remember that fathers form 50 per cent of parents and times should be chosen when they can attend. Not all of them finish work at 3.30: on the other hand some may do shift work in the evenings. If the amount of time spent on this exercise seems inordinate remember that parents, in the long run, will exert more influence on their children's development than even the best teacher.

SCHOOL MAGAZINE

This can form a welcome link between school and parents and can also be a useful teaching point for lessons and activities. Why not invite parents to contribute to the articles, which can include programmes of events, information on developments and changes in staff and buildings, organisational and curriculum changes, expeditions and school success in sport, cycling proficiency etc, and examples of children's work?

SCHOOL FUNCTIONS

The range of activities to which parents can be invited is endless – sports, music, carol festivals, plays and so on. The only danger is that the audience becomes more important than the performance. A slick production is all very creditable but parents should understand that they are seeing the culmination of primary school learning activities and not a performance by the Royal Shakespeare Company.

PERSONAL SUPPORT

There are many ways in which individual parents can support the school and at the same time feel that they are partners in education. These include contributing materials, expertise on building projects, clerical and non-teaching chores, supervision of swimming pool or playground and serving on governing bodies. Corporately parents can be encouraged to organise money-raising and social activities including bazaars, fêtes, raffles, jumble sales, dances, and second-hand shops.

A school with a dynamic and balanced programme for encouraging and controlling parental cooperation will probably be working well in other respects. If there is distance between school and parents the task of the teacher in the classroom will be made that much more difficult.

The educational community

It is sometimes more common for a school to ignore the educational community outside its own gates than it is for it to ignore parents. What is happening in other schools and institutions is bound to exert an influence on the school decision-maker, even if he is unaware of it. Keeping in touch with this community is the very least that should be done.

Most headteachers meet fairly regularly with their primary school colleagues, and perhaps less often with their secondary colleagues. Such meetings can be very useful forums for discussing problems and initiatives but they sometimes go little further than being mutual support groups for discussing organisational or transfer difficulties. The kernel of school life is the curriculum so time should be set aside to debate with one's colleagues the pros and cons of adopting a particular pattern. Discussions on these lines with secondary colleagues is especially helpful in promoting increased understanding about what each sector is trying to achieve.

More than isolated discussion is necessary however. School visits and exchanges should be encouraged. Teachers are, by and large, a conservative group and often find it difficult to accept even fellow professionals in their classrooms, but it is surprising how much can be achieved by a joint exploration of a problem and ways of solving it. The problem of time and class disruption can make such exchanges difficult to achieve but if they are carefully planned, organised, and evaluated they can be a source of strength to individual teachers and promote inter-school harmony.

Schools outside the primary sector should not be forgotten. Exchanges with secondary schools can often be arranged after the Whitsun half-term, and this can be particularly beneficial to the primary school leavers. The opportunity to let the children meet some of their new teachers should be taken if offered, or even better they should be taken to the secondary school to see a play, school sports or possibly share in PE or home economics lessons. Ways of enabling parents to see something of the secondary school before transfer should also be explored.

How many primary heads know what is offered in a tertiary college or college of further education? Yet these institutions are influential in shaping the education system itself and the eventual life style of their students. Lecturers in FE can be heard criticising 'modern methods' when their most recent direct knowledge of a primary school was 1940, or secondhand when their children attended in 1960. Why not arrange to visit your local college and encourage some two-way interchange of ideas? The spin-off in expertise suddenly made available to you from both staff and students could be surprising.

Special schools have already been mentioned. It is a salutary experience to visit a hospital school for the mentally handicapped or a residential school for the visually impaired. These schools are part of our education service and as such all primary heads should at least have some knowledge of their functioning. Many of these schools will be developing as resource centres to help ordinary schools with special problems, while visits to them may open up new career opportunities for teachers in mainstream education.

Some of the most common 'whipping boys' of the education service during the seventies were the colleges of education. Newly qualified teachers who could not keep discipline, had no idea of how to teach literacy and numeracy, and were themselves poor spellers – these complaints were com- monplace. There may well have been an element of truth in these allegations as colleges tried to come to terms with rapidly reducing intakes after ten years of unparalleled expansion. Most of the comments were pretty subjective however and few heads went to the trouble of checking the actual situation in the colleges. Take the opportunity therefore of visiting your local college, or joining an in-service working party, and if you are still dissatisfied with the product of the college tell them so from a position of real knowledge.

The importance of good links with playgroups has been emphasised. Not only will this provide a useful forum for making contact with parents but it will also be directly helpful to the playgroup supervisor and her staff, provided that the impression of the school making a takeover bid is avoided.

The wider community

It might be thought that local businesses and industries are more relevant to secondary schools. Despite this, and welcome moves to improve liaison between secondary education and industry, the primary school still gets its share of criticism from the world of work. We are constantly being told that the basic skills are not being taught or that all would be well if we took a leaf out of the industrial managers' book. The only way to overcome these difficulties in communication is to invite the critics to see for themselves, and to go and visit them. The response will probably be mixed – some firms will ignore you completely but others may be keen to enter a period of close collaboration which will be of benefit to both sides.

Using the media, press, radio and television is an art in itself. Some authorities employ public relations officers and they can offer sound advice on what is possible and what should be avoided. Nothing can be more boring or irritating than seeing one school constantly in the headlines, presenting proficiency certificates, winning swimming shields, having its fête opened by the Prime Minister. On the other hand good but balanced press relations can be a great advantage if a problem should ever arise at your school which might involve adverse comment.

Establishing strong relationships with the world beyond the school is time-consuming. Care obviously has to be taken not to undervalue the basic needs of the school. However, those needs are likely to be better met if a carefully planned community programme is operated. In the rapidly changing eighties, with micro processors bringing a new industrial revolution and a changing work ethic, no school can afford to ignore the wider community. Everything should be done to gain an understanding of that community and to encourage it to be understanding about the primary school's own objectives.

11 Routine Administration

The distinction between management and administration has already been made. Management is concerned with decision-making, administration with implementation. Much of this book has been concerned with making heads aware of the context within which they manage, of the constraints upon their freedom, and of the measures likely to produce an atmosphere that will maximise the chances of successful management. Nevertheless administration itself is important as the most carefully designed plans can flounder if not properly administered.

There is the very real danger that administrative tasks assume too much significance or else are almost completely ignored. This seems more frequently the case in the small rural school where a head has to manage his time to cope with both a full timetable and administrative tasks. Carefully thought-out procedures are therefore needed to keep the paperwork in hand without it being relegated to the waste paper bin. Equally important is an attitude of mind which recognises that administration is part of successful educational management and not something beneath a head's dignity.

It is possible to identify the main components of good administration which can then be applied in the appropriate circumstances. Standard procedures are needed so that confusion and mistakes are avoided. If the administrator knows what is required to achieve a certain action it is less likely that in an emergency an important detail will be forgotten. Such procedures will also ensure a continuity of action and avoid 'one-off' reactions to sudden demands and requests.

Clear channels of communication and consultation will be

established by sound administration. If everyone has clearly defined responsibilities, and is aware of them, school life will function smoothly and teaching will be efficient. Good administration will take care that skills are used properly, that time is devoted to key tasks and not to irrelevant operations, and that energies are used in the right places. Above all the administration will be organised so as to be unobtrusive, *serving* teaching rather than constraining it, and flexible, meeting situations appropriately with planned responses but with the capacity to adapt.

If the planned use of procedures is important in relation to paperwork and manpower, so too are they in relation to time. Administration should be concerned with spreading the workload of the school effectively both in day-to-day activities and in more unusual circumstances.

Planning the hall and television timetables are examples of the day-to-day activities. Not only is it necessary to be fair to all classes, but also to ensure that the time spans are appropriate to the age group and activity being pursued and that, for instance, a thirty minute hall period is not followed immediately by a twenty minute television programme. The allocation of time is perhaps one of the most important functions of the head as an administrator.

Avoiding a clash of dates, or a conglomeration of activities at the same time, are functions of good administration. In many primary schools the end of term sees a rush of activities many of which could easily have been spread over the previous weeks. Sometimes these dates are not even placed in diaries and often all that is done is to place them on a convenient year planner in the staffroom. However, with a little more thought a flow chart or critical path diary can be prepared and time problems seen at a glance. Particularly helpful is a chart which shows the classes involved at any particular time. An example is shown overleaf. Different colour shading can be used for each class.

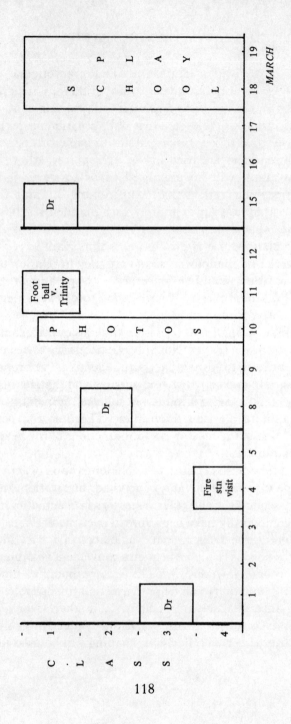

Procedures, communication and planning of time will all improve a school's administration but there still remain some key areas where a little thought will pay an excellent dividend.

Information

The passing of information is often done lightly with little thought about procedures or timing. First of all decide what different types of information are most needed in the school, who needs the information and when is it needed. The most likely recipients are staff, children and parents. Can the information safely be delivered orally and individually or are more standard procedures appropriate? Should it be given out in assembly or at a staff meeting or will a circular have more effect?

Parents should be, and need to be, kept well-informed about special activities or particular problems at school. Often this saves misunderstanding or even ill-will later. The information must be carefully presented. It is unlikely that parents will bother to read to the end of a two-page, closely typed and poorly duplicated letter. The information should be clearly sub-headed and relate to what parents need to know. Too much detail leads to boredom, too little to confusion. The letter should be worded so as not to insult the readers' intelligence but, at the same time, should take into account the reading limitations of some parents. It should not be written in official jargon but it should avoid being too chatty and informal. The head should keep a file of all circular letters sent home and a simple numbering system on the letters can be a help also to any bureaucratic minded parent.

Information for children can either be presented directly to them at the conclusion of morning assembly or can be delivered via a note to class teachers. Most heads will have their own views about the sanctity of assembly but many will want to take advantage of this communal time to present information which is of value to the whole school. Provided this is kept in check it should not upset the religious aspect of the assembly.

From time to time, however, recourse has to be made to the traditional note sent to the classes. There are some fairly obvious points to watch. A simple ticking system on the note will make sure that each class has received it and it will be particularly necessary to observe this if the missive concerns the supervision of children. Before the note is sent be absolutely certain that it is necessary. Nothing is more infuriating than to break off a story, the explanation of a maths concept, or a scientific experiment, to read a note which could have been left until playtime. Many heads find that sending an exercise book round containing the notes, each one dated, is a better system than using separate pieces of paper.

The staffroom notice board (if your school is fortunate enough to have one) should be the centre of the information system. Too often, however, the board is a jumble of out-of-date notices, often completely irrelevant to the running of the school. Thought, therefore, should be given both to notices and the board.

Notices should be attractive, readable and, if important, eye-catching. If they are not important should they be on the board at all? A simple colour banding system can identify the main categories of notice, eg, orange hatching for in-service training announcements (which frequently never get past the head), blue hatching for teaching vacancies, red hatching for PTA news.

The board itself should be kept in a tidy state. Notices of similar categories should be kept together and out-of-date ones removed and kept in a simple filing system in the staffroom. One part of the board could be labelled TODAY or THIS WEEK and reserved for the most immediate notices. Some large and long-term notices such as BBC and ITV timetables could perhaps be removed to another place completely.

The running of the staffroom noticeboard is an ideal task for delegation to a teacher with a flair for design and order. This teacher could also be responsible for keeping the school's other information systems up to date, including the staff handbook, fire precautions, etc.

Finally·if the staffroom is used as it should be, as part of the information system, it is important that every teacher visits it at least once during the day. They should be encouraged to have their mid-morning coffee there with their colleagues and not in the isolation of their own room.

Forms

When administration is discussed at heads' meetings the mind immediately leaps to the vexed question of forms. Most heads would agree that there are too many and that most of them are useless. As always there is a mixture of truth and exaggeration in this. However, if the filling in of forms is seen as a time-consuming and unnecessary exercise there is something wrong with the head's attitude, his procedures, or external demands upon him, and the reasons should be sought.

Forms mainly originate from one of three places: the DES, the LEA, or the school, with the LEA probably being the biggest offender. Forms seek information to ensure that manpower is being used efficiently and rewarded suitably, to ensure that statutory procedures are being carried out, or to elicit information which may be of help in improving the service. If the reason for having the form is understood a head is more likely to cooperate in filling it in.

Forms from the DES are not all that frequent, the most common being Form 7, upon which much of the statistical information about the nation's education is based. DES and NFER questionnaires are sometimes sent to primary schools and despite the chore involved it is worth filling them in carefully because the evidence produced can well have a long-term effect on educational planning.

It is the LEA forms which generate the most friction. Sometimes they seem unrelated; they are frequently changed. Nil returns are requested which may seem counter-productive. Many LEA forms are required to ensure that the authority is carrying out its financial commitments responsibly, including the payment of teachers. The forms should allow the local government administration to meet the demands of the auditor but most education departments will listen sympathetically if you question the need for a form. Most people working in local government are as disenchanted with forms as headteachers.

Like the DES some LEA forms ask for information on how well the service is functioning as one of the steps towards making improvements. This evaluation process may be time-consuming, and when several questionnaires arrive together it can be aggravating, but as we have seen it is an important component of management.

It is unlikely that the primary head will need to produce many forms but if he does there are a few golden rules:

1 Make sure that the information you want cannot be collected in a better way.
2 Be clear about the use to be made of the information collected.
3 Consult the customer about the design and be sure he understands the need for it.
4 Make it clear and concise, and if it is to be a repetitive form ask for returns with the longest possible intervals.
5 When the form has outlived its usefulness abandon it.

Procedures

The desirability of establishing sound and known administrative procedures has already been acknowledged in this chapter. Equally important is the setting of procedures dealing with the day-to-day life of the school. All teachers should be aware of the procedures for registration, dinner money collection and assembly. Procedures for dealing with more irregular happenings should also be made clear; what happens to children at wet playtime or lunchtime for example? It is far better to have a plan which can swing into action at the wave of a hand than to invite indecision and delay. Such procedures reduce the opportunities for confusion and indiscipline among children. They should be known and understood by all teachers and some schools might find the production of a simple staff handbook helpful provided it is updated when necessary.

Filing

All efficient administrators need a simple but effective filing system. The system should meet the demands of the school, so commercial systems should not be adopted without careful thought and adaptation. The main reason for having a filing system is, of course, to ensure that papers can be put away and then retrieved with a minimum of fuss and delay.

There are some common pointers to an effective retrieval system, whichever form of filing is eventually used. Precise definitions are important and although the number of files used should be kept to a minimum too wide a definition can easily lead to endless confusion. Each part of the system should be given a common number and the files within that part given an appropriate sub-number. Thus language development could be 40; staffing 60; accommodation 10; governors 50; and so on. Within one sector the system can be further divided:

60 Staffing – teachers	61 Staffing – non-teaching
60.1 Salary scales	61.1 Salary scales
60.2 Grouping documents	61.2 Canteen: establishment
60.3 Establishment	61.3 Cleaning: establishment
60.4 Advertisements	61.4 Advertisements

An index should be kept of the filing system, available to all who need to use it.

Sometimes effective use can be made of different colours for filing purposes which increases the speed of identification. However, when a new system is started begin in pencil so that adjustments can be made in the light of experience and errors and omissions corrected. For the same reason gaps should be left in the numbering system so that new files can be inserted without upsetting the number sequence.

One of the functions of a good clerical assistant, or school secretary, even if part-time, should be the maintenance of the filing system. If the part-timer's hours are properly arranged filing should not wait too long. It does help if the head, when passing paper on for filing, marks a clear 'F' at the top of the paper, and gives some indication of the appropriate file to be used. This is perhaps the proper point to move on to the key to successful administration.

The school secretary

It is clear that a number of local authorities undervalue the assistance given to a school by a secretary, or, as she is more often called in the primary school, the clerical assistant. Only the largest primaries have one available full-time and smaller schools may have to make do with help on only one or two mornings each week. If more clerical help was available it would reduce the routine administrative load on the head and free her for the more professional duties of management and teaching.

However, even when a school has a reasonable allocation of clerical hours the secretary is not used as effectively as she should be. Too often her only basic task is dinner money and register collection and the rest of her time is taken up with items that tend to arise on the spur of the moment. A well-thought-out job description is, therefore, a must and the exercise of doing this will force the head to appraise the use that is made of his secretary.

A good secretary can be one of the most effective public relations officers a school has. She should be well-turned out with a pleasant manner. This is especially necessary for dealing with parents, for some of whom a visit to the school is still little better than a trip to the dentist. With more aggressive parents a sympathetic secretary can often calm ruffled edges before the head's door is reached and in many cases the problem can be solved without recourse to the head. On the other hand, it is important that the secretary does not act as an immovable object between visitor and head but as a flexible and helpful mentor to both.

If the secretary is to perform this function properly her siting is important. Clearly the design of the school, the space available and heating arrangements all constrain where a secretary can be accommodated. However, a careful analysis of the available space may yield some surprising results. It is unsatisfactory for a secretary to share the head's room unless this is inescapable; he, or she, does not want to be disturbed by the typewriter; the secretary does not want to be sent out every time a confidential visitor arrives. It is equally unsatisfactory if visitors have to run the gauntlet of remedial room, staff toilets and staffroom before coming to the secretary's office.

Whenever possible, therefore, the secretary should be sited near to the main entrance, in a space of her own, and with a clear sign welcoming visitors. If her office is enclosed a sliding window system can do a lot to provide a more intimate relationship with the visitor. If a separate office is unavailable a welcoming reception area could be made in the entrance hall, or a cloakroom adapted to serve as a reception concourse. The equipment needed actually at a secretary's fingertips is not as great as sometimes imagined. In harsh financial times LEAs will not be keen to spend money on administrative accommodation but the wise head, in his bid for a minor works allocation, will emphasise the advantages accruing to the professional side of the school.

An efficient secretary, given the opportunity and invited to use her initiative, can make the head's task easier in many small ways. As a 'telephone sifter' she can answer many queries herself, passing to the head those which he should deal with. Files can be made ready in advance of meetings, and papers arranged for conferences. Not only will this save time but it will promote an air of efficiency in the school. She will also know when the head can be disturbed and when not; quite reasonably most heads want to make themselves available to children but there are times when a stretch of peace and quiet is essential.

If the secretary is part-time a profile of the week's pressure points should be established and arrangements made for her to attend at those times; if necessary messages and letters can be stored on a dictaphone to await her return. Her secretarial tasks should also be specified; is it her job to make the staff their morning coffee and wash up after them? Should she always be the one to run off carol sheets on the duplicator or should a teacher in charge of audio-visual aids accept this as one of his or her responsibilities?

The secretary is close to the main holder of authority in the school and she is often among the longest serving members of staff of the establishment. This probably means that some reflected authority is invested in her. This can lead to a situation of potential conflict, for while the secretary is seen as professionally junior to any member of the teaching staff her central place in the organisation can sometimes lead to a contradiction of this relationship. Provided heads recognise this danger it can be avoided with tact and sensitivity.

Day-to-day administration

One of the most difficult tasks facing any headteacher is how to cope with the multitude of day-to-day problems that face him or her, and how to leave time for the really important decisions; in short, how to sort the wood from the trees. Any single day can bring decisions or actions on stock ordering, room allocation, supply teachers, difficult parents, maintenance, the education officer, school meals, in-service training, curriculum development, transport – to name only a few. How can the head deal with the administrative priorities and leave herself time for management?

Running an efficient administrative structure through the filing system, use of secretary and so on, as discussed above, is part of the answer. So is knowing how to deal with the letters and other pieces of paper; which ones need an immediate answer, which can be referred; which items can be dealt with on the telephone, which need further research?

Broadly speaking a headteacher has four main perspectives: her role as the main curriculum developer and evaluator in the school; her personnel role; her tasks as community relations and public relations officer; and her role as resource provider. It is obvious that few problems will be exclusive to one category but it may be useful to identify the main category to which an individual situation belongs. Without realising it a head may be concentrating on the task of curriculum developer at the expense of the personnel needs of the school. Staff tensions will build up and these will create further problems to reduce overall the time available for management.

Research tends to show that heads are either people-orientated or process-orientated. Thus one style of headship can be very different from another. A basic difficulty for both types is freeing oneself from the small decisions which it is necessary to take. The only answer is delegation and this involves a careful review of school objectives combined with job evaluation and description.

Delegation

Some administrative problems can be referred upwards to someone of a higher status, the chief adviser or the chief education officer. Other items can be deferred as the head decides that although action may be necessary its immediacy is not essential. Sometimes the item is deferred while further information is sought. This leaves items which must either be dealt with by the head or delegated.

Delegation is a power which most managers are afraid to use to the full. However, the advantages can be considerable, freeing time for the head, involving a subordinate in higher status work and, not infrequently, arriving at a better decision from someone closer to the problem.

How far down the line should the delegation be pushed? Deputy head, secretary, Scale 1 teacher, caretaker? This depends on three things:

1 At what point does the person in the line have access to all the information necessary to tackle the job? For instance, a probationer cannot be expected to make a judgement on the introduction of a new reading scheme.
2 At what point can the person delegated decide what is best for the whole school? Tied up with this is the question of status, one of the differences that we have seen between educational management and business management. Can a Scale 2 teacher with responsibility for language development make operational decisions about the annual school play, or should these be made at a higher level?
3 Can the individual exercise good judgement on the item in question?

The first two criteria are easy to apply but the last one is difficult and involves staff appraisal. However, when the decision to delegate is made the incumbent should be given the resources to complete the job and the terms of reference should

128

be clearly understood by all concerned. Avoid the temptation to think you could do the job better yourself; you probably could but can you use your time better? – that is the crucial question. Finally allow the person doing the job the chance to show his initiative; this is not the same as abrogating responsibility.

Am I effective?

One way of deciding whether your routine administration is effective is to compare what you think you do with what happens in practice. If your answers to the following questions are 'no' you are spending too much time on administration and not enough on management.

1 Do you organise your week and day according to predetermined priorities?
2 Are you balancing out your time efficiently between the main aspects of the job?
3 Are you giving adequate time to reviewing the past, evaluating the present and planning for the future?
4 Are you doing only that work which cannot be delegated?
5 Are you seeing all the people you should be seeing, including non-teaching staff?
6 Are you able to complete tasks?
7 Are you making time for your own professional improvement through reading and in-service education?
8 Are you keeping in touch with what is happening in the classrooms in your school?

12 The Small Primary School

Most of this book is applicable to primary schools whatever their size. Each school has its own particular circumstances and environment which make it unique. The needs of the inner city primary school are very different from those of the school in the wealthy suburbs of a country town. Less often recognised are the problems of managing the smallest of primary schools, often situated in an isolated village community.

The thought of being head of such a school, with few staff to control and a small number of children to worry about, situated in the middle of beautiful countryside, may seem appealing to the teacher grappling with remedial problems in Birmingham or Manchester. The truth can be very different, for running such a village school has its own particular difficulties.

The school may have fifty children on roll, staffed by a head and one assistant. The children will be divided into two classes, infant and junior, with a wide spread of ages in each. The head might be supported with five hours' clerical assistance and seven hours' cleaning time, but inevitably this support will not be available when it is most needed. Much of the head's time may be spent therefore on non-teaching or non-managerial duties. The building is likely to be small and old, and it may be difficult to organise the environment to suit modern teaching techniques.

The small school faces a number of difficulties which can restrict the curriculum and the development of the school, including the head's personal training. The amount of money available through capitation will restrict the equipment and resources available to the small school, although more enlightened authorities attempt to bolster small schools' capitation with a special allowance. The lack of contact with other adults in the school will mean that the primary head will not be able to test new ideas or activities against other people. It is quite likely that the nearest other primary school is several miles away.

The particular difficulties of the small school head are time, resources and contact.

The newly-appointed head will quickly discover that, in a small school, he must be an administrator, a manager, a leader and organiser, and a manual worker, at the same time as being a full-time teacher. Immediate solutions could be to stay at school later than usual, to take work home, to arrive at about 8.00 am or to double up classes if possible for certain periods of the week.

The last suggestion is rarely practical, nor in the children's interests, so most heads are forced into a combination of working late and early. Fortunately many authorities now provide some part-time teaching help for the small school and this can be used in a number of ways to make the head's task easier and more effective.

The most straightforward use of the part-timer is to relieve the head of teaching responsibilities, freeing him for other things. This can certainly be helpful for part of the week but other ways of using part-time help in the interests of the whole school should be considered. The part-timer might be able to extract small groups of children for special help or might offer a particular speciality to groups of children. One problem in a small school is to establish a wide but balanced curriculum with only a small number of adults. It is important therefore for all strengths to be fully used and the part-timer should be considered as much more than a child minder for the head's class.

If, however, the head has been able to plan the timetable of the school to give himself a free afternoon he must consider very carefully the most effective ways of using it. Teachers are professionals and they recognise that there are certain tasks which can be done after school hours when the children are not present. Few headteachers would maintain that their job is only from 9 am to 3.30 pm for 190 days a year. Time free from teaching in the small school will therefore be used most effectively in tasks which require the presence of children or other members of staff.

This time might be profitably spent in working with individual children, by team-teaching with a colleague as part of a staff development and in-service training programme, or by visiting neighbouring schools to make contact with colleagues and see them in action. The evaluation of children's work and teaching programmes could also take place during this time.

It is quite natural when a school has only a head and one assistant teacher, for them to assume that their teaching is complementary and that there is no need for written aims and objectives. What is discussed in formal meetings in larger schools can be sorted out over a cup of tea at lunchtime in the smaller school. One must of course have a reasonable attitude to consultation in the small school but the danger of assuming things will happen without proper consideration must be avoided. Even if the sessions only involve two teachers, time should be set aside for planning work and setting the objectives of the school.

All schools, whatever their size, need a basic amount of equipment and this can be a severe strain on the resources of the smaller primary school. Thought could therefore be given to jointly purchasing a piece of equipment and sharing its use with colleagues, on a mutual help basis. This idea need not be restricted to equipment. Arrangements could be made to share and exchange teachers who can offer specialist subjects to children or expertise to other colleagues.

The likely development of special schools as resource centres should not be ignored. Many secondary schools are anxious to improve contacts with primaries and they may have equipment, resources and even staff that can be borrowed.

Every opportunity should be taken for teachers in small schools to meet together, despite the practical difficulties, for in-service training and the sharing of ideas. Teachers will also want to maximise the use of voluntary help in the village to help with the one hundred and one tasks which are necessary to keep the small school running.

The most frustrating thing for the headteacher of a small school is the constant disruption of his teaching programme, even if he has managed to timetable himself some 'free' time. There are a number of things which can be done to minimise these disruptions. Parents can be contacted and asked to call before morning school or after school closes in the afternoon. Exceptions can be made for real emergencies but otherwise parents should not be allowed to disrupt teaching. If other visitors arrive unannounced and want to see the head they should be asked to make an appointment, unless it is an emergency.

The telephone in a small school can be a lifesaver but it can also be an irritating nuisance. If it is in the classroom lessons will be interrupted while it rings and is answered. If it is elsewhere the class must be left while it is attended to. Regular callers could be asked to call before or after school, or during the head's non-teaching time. Telephone answering machines can also be hired at reasonable cost and it might be worth investigating the possibility of using one to solve some of the problems. Use of a tape recorder for dictation has already been suggested and this practice can be very useful for the head of a small school.

If the organisation and administration of a small school is carefully planned the job of the headteacher can be one of the most rewarding in the education service. It cannot however be thought of as a sinecure as it is without doubt one of the most demanding posts.

13 Putting It All Together

When you are aware of all the constraints which affect your management and decision-making powers, and realise the boundaries of your authority, you are ready to put together the processes which lead from the setting of overall aims to the realisation of objectives. Despite temptation I have not strayed into the field of curriculum planning as there are many books available which detail the ways in which areas of learning should be planned. No individual book could in any case do justice to every part of the primary curriculum as well as looking at general management. I have, therefore, been more concerned with considering the essential framework within which all planning, organising, controlling and evaluating can take place, including that central part of school management, the curriculum.

Chapter 2 has already discussed this general framework and subsequent chapters have looked at the background to management together with a consideration of how the framework can be applied to different parts of the organisation. It is now necessary to complete the management cycle by putting the parts together.

There are certain management techniques which are fashionable from time to time and then fall from favour. The basic concept in most of these is the breaking down of aims and objectives into carefully planned and achievable steps. If this is done in a primary school effective management can take place. Many of these techniques are much more applicable to industry, business or government than to a school but if their general philosophy is accepted, rather than a rigid application of the system, a useful structure can be established.

One of the more popular techniques has been that known as Management By Objectives (MBO) and this is perhaps the most useful one to transfer to primary school use. MBO was introduced during the late fifties and early sixties when industry, coming out of the post-war years of insistent demand, became more conscious of the problems of competition and the need to be cost effective. The technique was codified by writers such as Brucker who advocated the setting of objectives in terms of output, resources and production, and the managing of the organisation to achieve these objectives.

MBO is concerned with results. Within the organisation aims are translated into objectives and each individual knows what is expected of him and how he can contribute towards their achievement. By involving individuals in the setting of aims and objectives they become more committed to achieving them. Built into the technique is an evaluation and improvement function. Thus MBO requires a structure or organisation which gives clear definitions about what is expected but at the same time allows freedom and flexibility for individuals to operate. In an education system which is trying to reconcile structure with autonomy it can clearly be useful.

MBO should be seen more as a way of life than as a bureaucratic exercise. It would help however if you were to spend a little time with paper and pencil, as well as in discussion with colleagues, to identify the major management areas. The essential task is to set out what are sometimes known as the 'Key Result Areas'. These are the major areas which contribute towards the overall aims that you have set yourself. Such key result areas might include:

Curriculum;
Quality of teaching;
Allocation of capitation;
Buildings;
Communications.

Each key result area then needs to be subdivided into 'Key Tasks'. Communications might be broken down into the following categories.

Communications

Relations with: Parents;
Governors;
Other primary schools;
Pre-school provision;
Comprehensive schools;
Advisory and support services.

A simple standard of performance can then be set for each key task. You might, for instance, set yourself the objective of having at least three parents' evenings a term, sending home two newsletters and making sure that there is a clearly defined channel for parents to make their individual problems known to you. Once the performance standard has been agreed a system of evaluation and control should be established. This should be simple but it is human nature to ignore the obvious warning signs. In the example of the parental key task, an absence of complaints that parents were ill-informed about school activities would show that the standard of performance in sending home a newsletter was being met.

If it is to work properly such an analysis of key areas and functions must be undertaken regularly, say at least once a year. This will allow you to see whether your standard of performance is satisfactory and whether any improvements are necessary. This simple exercise has the advantage of concentrating the mind and can be used to good effect not only on direct curriculum areas but also in the management of non-teaching areas. The relating key tasks and areas to the overall aims will help to ensure that all the school's activities are pulling in the same direction.

Key Result Area and Key Task Area	Standard of Performance	Control and Evaluation	Improvements
5 Communications			
5.1 GOVERNORS	5.1.1 That governors are given sufficient information to fulfil their function efficiently including: (i) regular head's report (ii) response to individual enquiries.	5.1.1 Public comment, including staff and parents.	5.1.1 All parents to be given list of governors.
	5.1.2 That governors are made to feel part of the school by (i) visiting school; (ii) being invited to school functions.	5.1.2 Parents and staff know who governors are and what their function is.	5.1.2 Individual staff to be invited to attend governors' meetings to speak on curriculum.
	5.1.3 That the governors adequately represent the school at the LEA and in the community.	5.1.3 Head can rely on governors for support at difficult times.	
5.2 PARENTS	5.2.1 That parents are welcomed into the school.	5.2.1 Parental worries are brought to head and do not build up.	5.2.1 Tell all parents of time when head will be free to see them at short notice.
	5.2.2 That parents are kept informed by newsletter.	5.2.2	
⟶	5.2.3 ⟶	⟶	⟶

PART OF AN MBO ANALYSIS

137

Evaluation

The difficulties of measuring achievement in the education world have already been noted in Chapter 2. Despite this any public activity that is so expensive and so central to the future survival of the nation must at least attempt to monitor its success or otherwise. This can be done at a number of levels.

The LEA will be very concerned to get value for money and to be sure that money is being spent in the most effective way. This may mean attempting to evaluate the outcome of improving the pupil–teacher ratio instead of increasing capitation allowances. At the school level a primary head, although he or she may have to make similar judgements over the use of virement, will be more worried about measuring individual children's progress and the general success of the school.

It is as well to be aware at the outset that different groups will measure output and success in different ways. What might be very desirable from a teacher's point of view might be completely irrelevant for a parent. Thus any measurement of success must take this into account.

The Green Paper presented to Parliament in 1977 by the Secretary of State for Education and Science read:

> The challenge now is to restore the rigour without damaging the real benefits of child centred developments . . . teachers need to identify with some precision the levels of achievement represented by the children's work. Teachers can plan a progression in these parts of the curriculum and so ensure that they make their proper contribution to the child's education. Teachers should, as a matter of professional habit, pass on clear information about work done and levels of achievement.

If a clear structure has emerged from consideration of the management of the curriculum teachers should still be free to guide each child at an appropriate pace using their favoured materials and methods. It will, however, be possible for a system of recording to be devised to show each child's progress through the structure. Some LEAs have therefore formalised record-keeping for the basic skills of mathematics and language development and have formulated guidelines to assist teachers in planning for individual progression by identifying more clearly where a child is at any particular moment, and where his next step should be. However, whatever LEA or DES guidelines or assessments are produced, the best evaluator must remain the individual teacher who should be trained to diagnose and prescribe within the agreed framework.

Whatever system of evaluation and record-keeping is used the keynote should be simplicity and effectiveness. It will be of no use whatsoever if all a teacher's time is taken up with writing notes about progress. The record will certainly not be read by future staff if five pages are used to state what could be said in one. Record-keeping should therefore be geared to evaluating the child's progress (and much of this can be done by keeping a record of the child's own work) with a view to knowing where to go next.

By putting together teachers' evaluations of their progress you as head will be able to establish whether or not you are meeting the aims which have been set. Aims which are not appropriate to record-keeping and class assessment will have to be monitored in other ways and the standard of performance you set yourself will determine to a large degree the method of evaluation. Leaving to one side the topical argument about accountability, nothing can be improved without prior evaluation. If the management cycle is to be completed this vital part must not be omitted, no matter how difficult or imprecise it is.

Postscript

The aim of this book has been to assist new primary headteachers in every-day management situations, to introduce them to basic techniques and to place them and their schools in the total educational context. No easy solutions have been offered for it is only the individual head, in his or her own school, who reach the solutions. But I have suggested basic principles and practices which, if taken together, will avoid the often fatal results of inconsistent and off-the-cuff decisions.

The task of a primary headteacher is exacting. He or she must be a good teacher, an excellent organiser, an innovator and a motivator, a public relations officer and a confidant. Above all he must balance the conflicting pressures which are constantly upon him, retain a sense of humour and get on with people. There can be few careers as depressing as teaching for those who cannot meet these high demands, but there can be few as rewarding for those who can rise to the challenge. It is quite right that all the evidence points to the fact that the major determinant of a school's achievement is the quality of the headteacher but it is also a great responsibility to bear. With careful planning, organisation and management the burden should be made more bearable.

14 An A – Z

Admissions

The LEA decides on the procedure for admitting children to school, including the age at which they may start and for which resources will be provided. The law requires that children must be admitted no later than the beginning of the term following their fifth birthday. It is usual for heads to be consulted, and the actual routine for making the admission is nearly always delegated to them, but the LEA retains control. The governors of voluntary aided primary schools are responsible for their admissions, although it is expected that this will be in accordance with arrangements agreed with the LEA over such matters as zoning. Actual admissions will be done by the head but he will be answerable in this case to the governors.

Parents can insist on a school place for a child of statutory age but they cannot insist on a particular school. A place is not guaranteed until the child's name appears on the admissions register.

Sometimes a school attempts to refuse admission to a youngster on the grounds that he is not old enough to satisfy LEA admission policy, but if he has already been in full-time education elsewhere in the country then he must be admitted as full-time education must be continuous.

Break

LEAs rarely make local regulations about when breaks may be taken or for how long they may last. Heads are therefore responsible for the arrangements for break times although if these are unreasonable or unworkable the LEA may wish to intervene. Morning and afternoon playtimes count as part of the education session; lunch breaks which divide the sessions do not.

Heads are responsible for arranging adequate supervision throughout all breaks, and for ensuring that this supervision is carried out. It is regarded as insufficient to have someone 'on call'. The supervision must relate to the age of the children, the nature of the play area and any possible dangers that can be foreseen. Provided that these rules are followed, and all supervisors are adequately briefed, it is not necessary for the supervisors to be qualified teachers.

It is important that adequate arrangements are made to cover for the absence of any member of staff on playground duty.

Confiscation

It is as well to have a school policy on confiscation and to make sure that all members of staff follow it. It is easy to put a confiscated article in a drawer, forget about it, and then have lost it when Mrs Brown demands it back.

A teacher has a right to remove from a pupil any object which is dangerous or which is interfering with the general good management of the class. However, he then has an obligation to look after it and keep it safe from loss or damage. The article must eventually be returned in the same condition as when it was removed; the alternative is, to all intents and purposes, stealing. If the article is considered dangerous arrangements should be made to return it direct to the child's parents.

Health and safety at work

The Health and Safety at Work Act, 1974, came into force on 1 April 1975. The act is designed to ensure the health and safety of all working persons, and other persons, against risks arising from the activities of work. The act itself is a general enabling measure; subsequent regulations have the force of law.

The supervision of the requirements of the act is entrusted to the Health and Safety Inspectorate who have the power to prosecute. Inspectors have wide powers of investigation, and they may remove dangerous articles, instruct that certain activities cease, investigate records and serve improvements orders.

It is likely that detailed advice on the act will be provided to all schools by their local authority, including details of Health and Safety Policy Statements and the setting up of appropriate Safety Committees in consultation with trades union representatives. However, the following general points may be useful to primary heads:

SCHOOL POLICY
The head should seek to establish and maintain a safe and healthy environment throughout the school and its grounds, and establish safe working procedures for staff in the school. Similar arrangements should apply to pupils, parents, governors and any other visitors to the school who may be affected by the establishment's activities. Sufficient information and training should be available to ensure that staff and pupils avoid all undue risks. Health and safety should be considered as an integral part of the curriculum. Effective procedures should be laid down and followed in the case of fire, evacuation and accidents.

RESPONSIBILITIES OF THE HEADTEACHER
The head should coordinate the implementation of the approved safety procedures in the school, delegating where appropriate, but ensuring that the responsibilities and limits of such delegation are carefully specified. This coordination should include a regular review of practices, provisions and

possible hazards. Consultation with governors and the chief education officer will be necessary from time to time.

RESPONSIBILITIES OF CLASS TEACHERS

The act states: 'it shall be the duty of every employee while at work: to take reasonable care for the health and safety of himself and of other persons who may be affected by his acts or omissions at work, and as regards any duty or requirement imposed on his employer or any other person by or under any of the relevant statutory provision, to cooperate with him so far as it is necessary to enable that duty or requirement to be performed or complied with.' Teachers should therefore:

(a) exercise effective supervision of pupils and be aware of any emergency procedures;
(b) explain emergency procedures in language that young infant and junior pupils can understand;
(c) integrate all relevant aspects of safety into the teaching process;
(d) follow safe procedures personally.

The health and safety of pupils is the responsibility of the teacher in charge of them at the time, whether on school premises (including playgrounds or playing fields) or not.

PUPILS

Pupils should be supervised and instructed in safety matters appropriate to the activities, situation, weather conditions, their age, etc. They should observe standards of dress and behaviour consistent with safety and hygiene, and should be warned not to misuse things provided for their safety.

Hours of opening

Each school should have available a timetable setting out the hours of opening. DES regulations give LEAs the right to decide on the exact times for beginning and ending school but state that all schools for statutory age children must have two sessions per day, with at least three hours secular instruction for those under eight, and at least four hours for those over eight. Dinner and registration times are not counted towards the hourly total, but other breaks can be.

Children under statutory school age may be admitted on a part-time basis but otherwise a one session 'continental' day is contrary to DES regulations except in exceptional circumstances such as a strike by lunchtime supervisors to which the only alternative would be closure.

Articles of government will usually allow for variations in starting and finishing times in view of local circumstances but these must be agreed with the LEA. It is vital that school hours are kept rigidly once agreed as law cases have turned on whether a child was in the care of the school at a particular time. In *Barnes* v *Hampshire County Council* in 1969 the Barnes family was awarded damages against the LEA because their five-year-old daughter was dismissed five minutes early and was knocked down. Therefore even if a child brings a note as having to go early he should only be allowed to do so if he is met by an adult. A small point arising from this is to ensure that all school clocks are set at the *right* time, and at the same time.

Illness and injury

Schools should provide first-aid boxes at suitable points. These should be readily accessible and kept well equipped. The items in the box should be usable by any member of staff whether trained in first aid or not. The boxes should include:

blunt ended scissors;
bandages of various sizes;

cotton triangular bandages;
adhesive tape;
sterilised cotton wool;
sterilised dressings and safety pins;
mild antiseptic solution.

All teachers should have a working knowledge of first aid, and the opportunity should be taken by some to attend specialist courses run by bodies such as the Red Cross or St John's Ambulance Brigade. The names of teachers or other staff qualified in first aid should be made known to all staff and children so as to avoid delay in seeking treatment in the case of accidents.

If someone is ill or injured first aid should be given as far as skill permits. It is however only 'first aid' and expert help should be called for if more than this is required. When aid is given certain processes should be followed as a matter of course. The emergency must be diagnosed so the first step is to discover what happened, or what signs and symptoms of illness there are. The sick person should be made comfortable so that the treatment can be given.

The top priority in treatment must be, on the very rare occasions when it is necessary, to resuscitate and sustain life. The child must then be reassured to put him in a calmer frame of mind. This does not require the teacher to be funny or too sympathetic, as such a response can over-dramatise the situation. The fewer people present at this time the better, although in the case of an injury it can help for a couple of the casualty's friends to stay and chat to him.

If you are not sure what to do, and life is not at stake, it is better to do nothing and wait for the experts to arrive.

Information for parents

In November 1977 the Secretary of State issued a Circular

(15/77) on the question of information for parents. The purpose of the circular was to suggest to authorities that each school should have written information about the school and its place in the educational system available for parents and prospective parents. The sort of information which the Secretary of State considered should normally be made available to parents included:

1 Name, address and telephone number of the school, hours open, term dates, address and telephone number of LEA;
2 Names of head, senior staff, chairman of governors and parent governors;
3 Characteristics of the school: age range, county or voluntary etc (important to include here explanation of denominational schools);
4 Arrangements for parents to visit the school and meet class teacher (bearing in mind the difficulties of working parents and the desirability of involving both parents);
5 Other arrangements to keep parents informed of children's progress;
6 The number of pupils and the admission arrangements;
7 Arrangements for transfer to the next stage of education;
8 Arrangements for religious education and for exemption from it;
9 An indication of the normal teaching organisation and any comments on homework. Ideally this should include advice on the authority's arrangements for handicapped children, gifted children, etc;
10 Clubs and extra-curricular activities;
11 Details of school rules and procedures;
12 Whether school uniform is required and if so the approximate cost: otherwise an indication of the type of clothing which is acceptable;
13 Details of any parents' organisation;
14 Provision for school transport;
15 The LEA's arrangements for free meals, clothing, etc.

Some primary schools issue nothing in writing to new or prospective parents. Many will supply what is thought to be relevant information but this sometimes goes little further than the 'plimsoll bag and name tag' concept. It is probably fair to say that few schools provide a detailed brochure along the lines suggested by the Secretary of State, although the practice is on the increase in larger primary schools.

There is no guarantee that the brochure will be read by parents, but nevertheless they have a right to such information. The head should ensure that any information given is accurate and couched in terms easily understood by all parents rather than in the terms commonly used in the education service.

Job evaluation

Some local education authorities have adopted a job evaluation scheme to help determine the salaries of centrally based staff and non-teaching staff working in schools. These are usually based on the nationally negotiated scheme, but they may have local variations.

In essence job evaluation is concerned with the comparison of jobs by the use of systematic and formal procedures which decide the relative position of the jobs one to another in a wage hierarchy. It provides the evidence for deciding on a pay structure but in itself it cannot determine what the pay levels are.

A commonly used form of job evaluation in education departments is the points rating system. This analyses the job in a number of key factors such as supervisory responsibility, complexity, contacts etc, and allocates points to the employee for each factor. The total points score determines the position of the job in the hierarchy, and is then translated into a monetary value.

Job evaluation measures the job, not the job-holder. It offers a rational structure of pay and recognises particular skills and responsibilities needed in jobs. For management it forces a disciplined approach to personnel problems. A full job evaluation procedure is very time consuming and even the most detailed analysis cannot discriminate sufficiently for the more demanding or complex jobs.

Primary heads may well find themselves having to complete job evaluation forms with their non-teaching staff and this will involve a detailed analysis of the job description, no bad thing in itself. It will be essential that you understand the scheme adopted by your authority and you should ensure that you have been given adequate training and information.

The office

Early chapters of this book have described in some detail the workings of the education office. The primary head will frequently need to contact 'the office', either by letter or by telephone and sometimes this seems a time-consuming business. There are some 'tricks of the trade' that may help, although their application will of course vary.

TELEPHONING

Try to know who you need to contact for a particular item; this will save time in being passed from one officer to another. Most schools will have an internal office directory and this will help you determine the most appropriate officer. Ask for him by name and extension, as one extension may service several officers. Avoid saying 'I want to speak to someone about . . .'; that is the way to undertake a phone-in to half the department.

If you are calling in response to a letter ask for the extension at the top of the page, not for the person who signed it. The signator (often it is the CEO anyway) may be exercising his supervisory responsibility and may not have the detailed information you require. For the same reason avoid always going 'to the top'; someone lower down in the office may be able to help you more fully, and probably more quickly.

Senior officers are busy people: much of their time is spent in meetings or visiting schools, often to sort out one of your colleague's problems. Therefore be patient if you are trying to contact them. If someone else can help you, use them. If you can find out when the officer will return, call back. If the matter is really urgent (few things are) the officer's secretary, if he has one, can usually contact him fairly quickly.

Try to be sensible about when you telephone. It often seems to the primary head that 'the office' call him at the most inconvenient time, in the middle of assembly or just when he has started the afternoon storytime with the infants. In fact most officers try to call on routine matters at break times or after school and it is reasonable to ask them to do so. In return think about the best time to telephone the office. Although you may have finished your lunch at 1.00 pm and be ready to return to work, remember that schools take lunch early and 1–1.30 is probably the most deserted time in an education department. After 3.30 is a better bet and some authorities advise heads of certain days when officers and advisers are more likely to be available.

WRITING

Letters to the office will take time to arrive; they will take even longer to be replied to. There are some golden rules: address your letter to the CEO 'for the attention of . . .' and try to keep separate subjects on separate sheets of paper. The reasons for this are simple. The office will have a messenger system which takes post from tray to tray; by direct addressing you will avoid a clerk having to decide who is the most appropriate recipient. By keeping subjects separate you will ensure they go direct to the officer concerned and are not dealt with in rotation.

The education officer may have to contact his colleagues before he replies, and the reply must then be dictated, quite probably with an audio system. If a bulk posting system is used there may be several days' delay before the signed letter reaches you. This is no excuse for undue delay but helps to explain why immediate replies are not always possible.

VISITING
Occasionally headteachers will turn up at the education office and ask to see an adviser or officer, and will then be most surprised to learn that he is not available. It is always much safer, as well as more polite, to arrange an appointment beforehand. For the same reason if an officer or adviser calls on you unannounced while you are teaching, it is quite reasonable for you to ask him to call again.

Ombudsman

The Local Government Act of 1974 established Commissioners for Local Administration in England and Wales, commonly known as the Local Government Ombudsman. His task is to investigate allegations of maladministration, not complaints about an education authority's policy. All complaints have to be passed to him in writing by a member of the local authority concerned. A number of the complaints made against local education authorities concern the admission of children to schools and normally involve the administrative staff of the authority. However, headteachers, except those of voluntary aided schools, are considered 'officers of the authority', and should be careful when dealing with the public that they do not lay themselves open to a charge of maladministration of the authority's clearly specified policies.

At the moment any action concerning the conduct, curriculum, internal organisation, management or discipline of a school is excluded from the Ombudsman's powers. The 1978 Report of the Ombudsman questioned this exclusion: 'a complaint about allocation to a school can be investigated; a complaint about allocation to a form cannot. A complaint about the management of a children's home can be investigated; a complaint about the school attended by the same children cannot.' The commission is therefore suggesting that internal school matters should be within its jurisdiction, claiming that the present exclusions are illogical.

There seems little doubt that most use of the Ombudsman is made by the 'middle' classes. Complaints about alleged planning maladministration are the most common, while those concerning housing and social services are much less likely.

Records

Certain records are required to be kept by the DES and by the LEAs. It is important that these statutory documents should be carefully kept and entries made in ink. These records, or extracts from them, may be used as evidence in court and it is vital therefore that they should be accurate. The DES requires the following to be kept in every maintained or direct grant school:

an admissions register;
attendance registers;
a school log book;
a punishment book.

All cases of corporal punishment must be entered in the latter. The log book should be maintained during the life of the school and then offered to the County Archives. The other records must be kept for at least three years from the date of the last entry.

The log book forms a permanent record of events connected with the history of the school and the following should be included:

1 Reasons for closure of the school, significant absences, or a marked variation in the school routine;

2 The receipt of any LEA or DES report on the school;
3 Changes in the character of the school;
4 Changes in organisation, accommodation or curriculum;
5 Involvement of governors in school life;
6 Matters of moment relating to staff.

Supervision

Arrangements for the supervision of children and the responsibilities of staff arising from these arrangements should be known by everyone involved, including, where appropriate, pupils and parents. These arrangements should cover supervision at the beginning and end of the day, break times, the consumption of milk and medicines, the use of minibuses and contract transport, the use of swimming pools and the movement of children between different parts of the building. Parking of cars by staff, parents and visitors should be controlled.

Generally accepted practice, which has no legal backing unless specified by the local authority's regulation, is for teaching staff to accept responsibility for pupils for ten to fifteen minutes before morning school. A sensible head will not lock school gates against children but he will advise parents about the reasonable time for which the school can accept responsibility for the children's safety. Nothing should be said to suggest that pupils arriving before this time will be accepted willingly.

Similar practice should be carried out after school and the pupils, unless staying for an organised activity, should be expected to leave the premises within fifteen minutes of the end of the school day. A school will not be held responsible if a reasonable system breaks down because a parent fails to meet a child. At some time in their careers the majority of primary headteachers will be faced with a small child stranded at school because no one has collected him. A caring head will approach

153

the difficulty from a human rather than a legal point of view but the fact remains that, as long as the agreed system has been followed, the school cannot be at fault.

It is therefore essential that each school works out its own system of supervision appropriate to its particular circumstances.

Further Reading

Birley, D. *The Education Officer and His World* (Routledge & Kegan Paul, 1970)

Dunsire, A. *Administration: the Word and the Science* (Martin Robertson, 1973)

Glendinning and Bullock *Management by Objectives in Local Government* (Charles Knight, 1973)

Fowler, Morris and Ozga *Decision-making in British Education* (Heinemann/Open University Press, 1973)

Kogan, M. *Educational Policy Making* (Allen & Unwin, 1975)

Edmonds, E. *The School Inspector* (Routledge, 1962)

Kogan, M. *The Government of Education* (Macmillan, 1971)

Pratt, J. *Your Local Education* (Penguin, 1973)

Stanyer, J. *Understanding Local Government* (Fontana/Collins, 1976)

Barrell, G. *Teachers and the Law* (Methuen, 1979)

Boyle and Crosland *The Politics of Education* (Penguin, 1971)

Blackie, J. *Inspecting and the Inspectorate* (Routledge & Kegan Paul, 1970)

Regan, D. *Local Government and Education* (Allen & Unwin, 1977)

Kogan, M. *County Hall–LEA* (Penguin, 1973)

Baron and Howell *The Government and Management of Schools* (Athlone, 1974)

Barry and Tye *Running a School* (Temple Smith, 1975)

Taylor, P. M. *Purpose, Power and Constraint in the Primary School Curriculum* (Macmillan, 1974)

Times Educational Supplement Guide to Careers in Education

Index

157

INDEX

INDEX